Originally published in 1882 under the same title.

ISBN 9781941324929

SKETCHES FROM

Texas Siftings.

BY

SWEET & KNOX

ILLUSTRATED BY

W. H. CASKIE

2018
Copano Bay Press

PUBLISHER'S NOTE

For the first new title we've released since Hurricane Harvey tore through South Texas and uprooted our business, our lives, and destroyed so much of my childhood home of Rockport, I wanted to do something lighthearted and fun. We Texans have an extraordinarily strong sense of place. It's an integral part of who we are. After witnessing the destruction of so much of the Texas coast—from Rockport, clear on up to Beaumont—and how we handled it as a people, I felt like we deserved few chuckles.

This book is dedicated to everyone who stuck their neck out to help neighbors and strangers after Harvey. The only thing in the Texas breed bigger than our sense of place is our hearts.

—Michelle M. Haas
North Padre Island

THE DRUMMER

The drummer inhabits railroad trains. He is always at home on the cars. He also temporarily infests the best rooms in hotels. In winter he wears an ulster, with the surcingle hanging loose behind, and in summer a linen duster.

He is usually swung to a satchel containing a comb and brush, another shirt, a clean celluloid collar, and a pair of cuffs; also a railroad guide, and a newspaper wrapped around a suspicious-looking bottle. That is about all the personal baggage he carries, except a "Seaside Library" novel, and a pocket-knife with a corkscrew in the back of it. He has a two-story ironbound trunk containing "sambles of dem goots," which he checks through to the next town. He always travels for a first-class house—the largest firm in their line of business in the United States, a firm that sells more goods, and sells them cheaper, than any two houses in the country. He is very modest about

stating these facts, and blushes when he makes the
statement; but he makes it, nevertheless, probably as
a matter of duty.

He can talk on any subject, although he may not
know much about it, but what little he knows he
knows, and he lets you know that he knows it. He
may be giving his views on the financial policy of the
British government, or he may only be telling you of
what, in his opinion, is good for a boil, but he will do it
with an air and a tone that leaves the matter beyond
dispute.

He is at home everywhere, and he never seems out
of place wherever you find him, although we do not
remember ever to have found him in church. Sitting
on his gripsack at a way-station, waiting for a train
six hours behind time, and abusing the railroad of-
ficials from brakesman to president, with a profuse
and robust profanity that gives the air a sulphurous
odor for miles around, he seems in perfect keeping
with the surroundings. The scene would be as incom-
plete without him as a horse race without a yellow
dog on the track.

When the drummer gets into a railroad train, if
alone, he occupies two seats. One he sits on, and on the
other he piles up his baggage and overcoat, and tries
to look as if they didn't belong to him, but to another
man who had just stepped into the smoking-car and
would be back directly.

Drummers are usually found in pairs or quartets on
the cars. They sit together in a double seat, with a
valise on end between them, on which they play eu-
cher and other sinful games. When they get tired of
playing they go out into the smoking-car, where the
man who is traveling for a distillery "sets 'em up" out
of his sample-case, and for an hour or two they swap

lies about the big bills of goods they have sold in the last town they were in, tell highly-seasoned stories about their personal adventures, and exhibit to each other the photographs of the last girls they made impressions on. **9**

While the drummer is not ostentatiously bashful, neither does he assume any outward show of religion. His great love of truth is, however, one of his strong points, and he is never known to go beyond actual facts, except in the matter of excessive baggage. Regarding this, he will sometimes stretch a point until it will cover up two hundred pounds of a three hundred pound trunk. He is the only man who dares address hotel clerks by their Christian names. He knows every hotel in the country, and every room in every hotel. When he arrives by a late train he is first to get out of the 'bus and reach the clerk's desk, when he says to the clerk: "Hello, Charley, old fel, how are you? Got No. 16 for me?" And the clerk flashes his Kohinoor and a smile on him as he shakes his hand, pounds the nickel-plated call-bell, and shouts, "John, take the gentleman's baggage to No. 16."

In the dining-room the drummer is a favorite with the colored waiters, although he orders more dishes and finds more fault with the fare than other guests do. He does not believe the waiter when he tells him that the milk is all out, but sends him off to inquire farther about the matter, and while the waiter is gone he fills up his glass out of the blue milk in the cream-pitcher. He flirts with the chambermaids, teases the boot-blacks and plays practical jokes on the regular boarders. He goes to bed at a late hour, and sleeps so soundly that the porter wakes up the people for two blocks around, and shakes the plaster off the wall, in trying to communicate to him the fact that

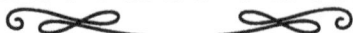

the 'bus for the 4:20 A. M. train will start in ten min-
10 utes.

The drummer has much to worry and fret him. Traveling at night to save time, sleeping in a baggage car
or the caboose of a freight train, with nothing but his
ear for a pillow, bumping over rough roads on stages
and buck-boards, living on corn bread and coffee din-
ners in crossroad hotels, yet under all these vexatious
circumstances he is usually good-humored and in the
best of spirits, although he sometimes expresses his
feelings regarding the discomforts of travel, and the
toughness of a beefsteak, or the solidity of a biscuit,
in language that one would never think of attribut-
ing to the author of Watts' hymns.

All kinds of improbable stories are told about drummers, some of them being almost as improbable as
the stories they themselves tell. For instance, we once
heard that a man saw a drummer in the piney woods
of North Carolina camping out under an umbrella.

"What are you doing here?"

"I am camping, and living on spruce gum to save
expenses," replied the drummer.

"What are you doing that for?"

"To bring up the average."

It seems that the firm allowed him a certain sum
per day for expenses, and by riotous living he had
gone far beyond his daily allowance. By camping out
under an umbrella and living on spruce gum for a few
days, the expense would be so small as to offset the
previous excess he had been guilty of. This story is
probably a fabrication.

The chief end and aim of the drummer is to sell
goods, tell anecdotes, and circulate the latest fashionable slang phrase. If he understands his business, the
country merchant might as well capitulate at once.

There is no hope too forlorn, nor any country merchant too surly or taciturn for the drummer to tackle. *11*
Our illustration at the head of this article shows the
country merchant under the influence of the drummer. That same merchant, not long ago, loaded up a
double-barreled shotgun with nails, with the intention of vaccinating the first drummer who entered
his store. The commercial emissary represented in the
picture has been talking to him only fifteen minutes.
In that time he has told the old man four good jokes,
paid him five compliments on his business ability and
shrewdness, propounded two conundrums, and came
very near telling the truth once. As a result, the san-
guinary old man is in excellent humor, and just about
to make out an order for $500 worth of goods that he
doesn't actually need, and then he will go out and take
a drink with the drummer.

The drummer is the growth of this fast age. Without
him the car of commerce would creak slowly along.
He is an energetic and genial cuss, and we hope that
he will appreciate this notice and the fact that we
have suppressed an almost uncontrollable impulse to
say something about his cheek.

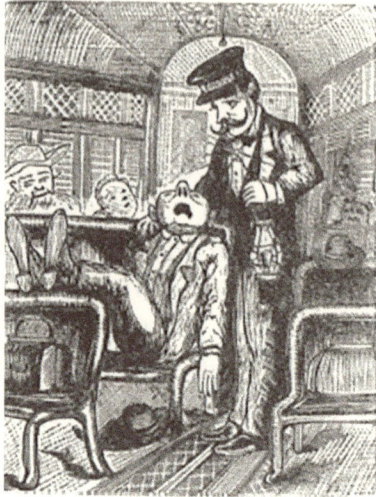

THE CONDUCTOR

In appearance, the conductor resembles a U. S.
Naval Officer. If a spy-glass were shoved under
his arm and he were taken up and set down on
the quarter-deck of a United States man-of-war, the
sailors would all think he belonged there. The only
difficulty about it is there is no United States man-
of-war it would be safe to put a conductor He would
not take any such risk of being drowned. Like the
captain of a ship, the conductor is boss of the situation. He does not precisely run the train. The engineer
does that, but the conductor runs the engineer. Unless
he chooses, he has no occasion to be civil to anybody
on the train, unless the president of the company is
on board.

The principal duty of the conductor is to take up
tickets, and collect fares from such as have neither
tickets nor passes. If any such passenger refuses to
pay, or attempts to put the conductor off, the conduc-

tor puts him right off in the middle of a big prairie. The conductor has even been known to treat newspaper men that way, and the journalist who is thus treated usually gets even by taking the conductor off—in his, the journalist's, paper. A journalist of that class will then proceed to denounce railroad monopolies.

As soon as the train leaves the station, the conductor enters the car, and after looking in out-of-the-way places for irresponsible parties who might be hiding, he proceeds to go through the car and to levy and collect assessments from the passengers, just the same as if he held a power-of-attorney from Jesse James himself. As a general thing, his authority to collect money from the passengers is only derived from Jay Gould, Vanderbilt, or some other legitimate highwayman. As it is very difficult for Jay Gould to be on every car in every train, and as the servant is like the master, passengers are directed to get their tickets before entering the car. The object of this is evidently to prevent passengers from paying their fares to the conductor, as he might not be able to bear up under the temptation. At night, however, the ticket-offices are not open, and the passengers have to pay their fares to the conductor, and then, if Jay Gould is not on the car, and if the conductor is not very conscientious, he may forget to turn the money over. Jay, himself, never forgets to turn the money over. When he buys a railroad cheap, he frequently turns it over three or four times, so they say.

Some passenger, who has a spite at a railroad company, makes a vow that the company shall never handle any of his money; so he always pays his fare to the conductor, and then he feels sure the company will never get any of it. The belief that railroad conductors grow rich in this way, is caused by many of them

wearing large diamond breastpins that outshine the
14 lantern the conductor holds on his arm. Very few people know that such breastpins cost only a dollar and a half at a hardware store, and are frequently presented to the conductors by drummers, as souvenirs.

Another duty of the conductor is to fail to impart information to reporters about any accident that may happen to his train. If a conductor tells a reporter anything about an accident, the company requests him to send in his resignation. Much more information can be obtained from a dead man, who has been run over, lengthwise, by five passenger cars, than can be got out of a conductor. When a reporter asks him for information about the dreadful accident, he talks and looks as if he relied on the reporter to tell him all about it.

In all seriousness, the conductor has combined a variety of qualifications to fill the position. He is, as a rule, very polite, considering the number of foolish questions that are put to him every hour in the day. He is courageous, and reliable, and above all, he is sober. When his varied qualifications, and the risks he runs, are taken into consideration, he is very poorly paid. It is estimated that one first-class conductor has more sense than a carload of legislators.

THE RAZORBACK HOG

To the traveler through Texas, one of the strangest and most peculiar features of the landscape is the razorback hog. He is of the Swiss cottage style of architecture. His physical outline is angular to a degree unknown outside of a text book on the science of geometry. His ears—or the few rags and tatters of them that the dogs have left—are furled back with a knowing, vagabondish air. His tail has no curl in it—although our artist has decorated him with one in the above illustration—but it hangs aft, limp as a wet dish-rag hung out of a back window to dry. The highest peak of his corrugated back is six inches above the level of the root of his tail. He does not walk with the slow and stately step of the patrician Berkshire, but usually goes in a lively trot. He leaves the impression that he was late starting in the morning and is making up for lost time; or that he is in doubt about the payment of that check, and is hurrying to get it cashed before the bank closes.

The country razorback prowls around in the woods and lives on acorns, pecan nuts and roots; when he can

16 spare time he climbs under his owner's fence and assists in harvesting the corn crop. In this respect he is neighborly to a fault, and, when his duty to his owner's crop will allow, he will readily turn in and assist the neighbors, even working at night rather than see the crop spoil for want of attention.

He does not know the luxury of a sty. He never gets fat, and, from the day of his birth, sometimes two years roll into eternity before he is big enough to kill.

Crossing the razorback with blue-blooded stock makes but little improvement. The only effective way to improve him is to cross him with a railroad train. He then becomes an imported Berkshire or Polan-China hog, and if he does not knock the train off the track, the railroad company pays for him at about the rate of one dollar a pound, for which they are allowed the mournful privilege of shoveling the remains off the track.

The ham of the country razorback is more juicy than the hind leg of an iron fire-dog, but not quite so fat as a pine knot.

The city razorback differs from his country relative only in the matter of the quality of his food and the length of his tail. The city species prey on the roots of tropical plants and other garden luxuries instead of corn, and eat cinders and old type in the back alley instead of the acorns and pecans of the breezy woodlands, that are assimilated in the digestive organs of the country *sus aper.*

The tail of the city hog has usually been chewed off in early life by dogs; in other words, it has been curtailed. This, and the arid patches on his back, where the hair has been scalded off by the enraged boarding, house cook, adds much to the picturesque appearance of the brute. A man once told us that the razorback hog was the only bird of prey that was amphibious in its habits, and that could lift a gate off its hinges without ruffling a feather.

As the novelists say, "much might be said on this very interesting subject," but time is money, and we are forced to conclude briefly with the following "pome" by one of the old masters:

Ye pigge he is a pretty fowl,
And wond'rous good to eat;
Hys ham is good, lykewise his jowl,
And eke his little feete.
But if you try a thousand yeare
I trow you still will fayle
To make a silk purse of hys eare
Or a wissel of hys tayle.

A COMPROMISE

A darkey entered Mose Schaumberg's store on Austin avenue, and asked the price of a hat, and was told the price was three dollars.

"I'll gib yer six-bits."

"Schon," said Mose to his clerk, "choost run dot tam darkey out of de store."

John seized the colored customer by the neck, and was shoving him out of the door, when the latter called out, "I'll gib yer a dollar. Speak quick before I quits de store."

"I takes your offer, mine frend. Pring him back, Schon."

ANOTHER
MYSTERY
EXPLAINED

You can see it down here in Texas already, and in a short time it will make its appearance all over the United States. Like prickly heat and boils, it comes out regularly every spring. We refer to the spectre of the front yard. Perhaps the reader does not quite comprehend our meaning. We refer to the woman who plants shrubbery and grubs about generally, every early spring, in her front yard—the woman's front yard, of course, not the spring's. Spring has not got any front yard of her own.

Early in spring the average woman, rich or poor, dresses herself in a faded calico dress, disguises herself in a big poke bonnet, and, armed with a garden rake, she goes prowling about like a scarecrow on wheels, a nigger with a watering-pot usually bringing up the rear of the procession.

The question arises: Why does the average female strive to make herself so hideous as to fill a dead man with distrust, if he were to walk past, when about the only returns for her trouble are a $40 rheumatic pain in her back, and a suggestion from her husband that she hire a wagon and go around selling vegetables? The reason why women will persist in fixing up a garden is simply because they cannot help themselves. They are acting from an irresistible impulse. As Guiteau would say, they are inspired to act as they do. We will try to explain what we mean.

Why do English sailors strip to the waist when the decks are cleared for action, and why is it, that when two Englishmen fight, the first thing they do is to pull off their coats? It is because their ancestors did. Julius Caesar says that when he landed on the coast of Britain, the natives divested themselves of their clothing before they rushed into the water to meet the Roman galleys. Perhaps the ancient Britons, like the modern editor, only had one suit and did not care to get it wet.

Why do stockmen of today brand calves that do not belong to them, and gobble up mavericks generally? Because it is in their nature to do so. The first stockman we read of, Jacob, played sharp tricks on Laban, his partner in the cattle-raising business.

Why, in the spring of the year, do picnics become epidemic, and old and young, rich and poor, rush off into the woods to eat their lunch under trees, and be fed on by ticks and mosquitoes? It is simply because for tens of thousands of years man was in a nomadic condition. He wandered about with his family in the woods, living on berries and being annoyed by insects, and although man has become civilized, and lives in a house, yet, nevertheless, about once a year an irresistible desire to return to his old vagabond life comes over him, and he just has to go on a picnic, after which he cools down for the rest of the year, and puts sweet oil on the tick bites.

Just so it is with women gardening. Until quite recently woman had to do all the hard work in the field. She had to dig up the ground, plant the crop and gather it, until it became second nature to her. Her husband was kind enough to encourage her to keep on by shaking a stick at her when she wanted to sit down and rest, but it was below his dignity to work.

Such was the condition of woman from the beginning
20 of time. It will be remembered that Adam was too
lazy to gather in the apples, so Eve had to do it for
him. Of course all this is changed now. All that most
women do in the way of hard work is to dress up and
go to parties; but every spring she cannot resist the
impulse to put on her worst clothes and drudge with
a hoe out in the front yard, as her ancestors used to
do thousands of years ago.

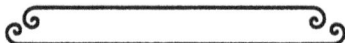

LITERARY ITEM

An Austin clergyman visited the jail a few days
ago, and asked one of the prisoners if he did not want
something interesting to read, offering him a tract
with the title "The Sinfulness of Gluttony."

The prisoner shook his head, and replied, "I've got
some reading matter that interests me more than
that."

"What is it?"

"Yesterday I had a copy of the indictment served on
me, and tomorrow I'm going to get a list of the jurors
that are to try me."

THE HOTEL CLERK

The hotel clerk is a young man who was originally created to fill an Emperor's throne or adorn a Dukedom; but when he grew up, there being fewer thrones and doms than there were Emperors and Dukes, he was temporarily forced to take a position behind a hotel register. His chief characteristics are dignity of bearing, radiant gorgeousness of apparel, haughtiness of manner, and jewelry. His principal duties consist in hammering on the call-bell, in handing guests the wrong keys to their rooms, and in keeping a supply of toothpicks on the end of the desk. When all his time is not taken up in the performance of these arduous duties, he will condescend to

explain to a guest that he does not know whether the
22 North-bound train leaves at 3 P. M., and if the guest
insists on enticing farther in, formation out of him,
he will probably hand him last year's official railroad
time-table.

When a stranger comes in on a late train, jams
his valise down on the counter and approaches the
register, the hotel clerk, in a preoccupied and austere
manner, turns the register and hands the stranger a
pen—a pen that has an impediment in its legs, catches in the paper, and splutters fragments of the guest's
name all over yesterday's "arrivals." The clerk, after
turning around the register and examining the signature to see if it is genuine, expresses some doubt as to
there being a vacant room in the house. The stranger
says he is bound to have a room. The clerk retires behind the desk, and after consulting some pigeon-holes,
concludes that the gentleman may have No. 1,192. He
writes some hieroglyphics on the register, and then
he talks for half-an-hour with the porter and the
baggage man about the trunk of the gentleman in
No. 46 having got mixed with the baggage belonging
to the gentleman in No. 64. When he gets that matter arranged he sits down to polish and admire the
long nail that he is cultivating on his little finger, and
forgets the gentleman who has rented No. 1,192, until
he is made aware of his existence by an impatient tap
on the counter. With the air of a martyr, and a sigh
that expresses the fact that he considers the whole
traveling public his enemies, he says, "Ah! would you
like to go to your room?"

There is about as much hospitality in his tone as
there is in the voice of a bull-dog when somebody
treads on his tail. It is not intended to be hospitable. It
is intended to impress on the mind of the stranger the

fact that, although he—the clerk—is passing poor on $12.50 a week and board, yet he is proud, and is mere- 23 ly filling the ignoble position he now occupies until he can come into his dukedom, which includes among its perquisites a yacht on the coast and a shooting lodge in the Highlands of Scotland.

Then John shows the gentleman to No. 1,192. No matter how crowded a hotel is, the hotel clerk always finds one room left for the late arrival. When the latter kicks about it, when he is leaving next day, because it was on the fifth floor, and was furnished with nothing but a bed, a bar of soap and a crack in the ceiling, the clerk tells him that if he had only been staying another day he could have had an excellent room— in fact, the best room in the house—which would be vacated after breakfast, by a gentleman who was leaving on the noon train. To our certain knowledge, the gentleman has been leaving that excellent—that "best room in the house"—every tomorrow for the last twenty years.

The hotel clerk is said to be distantly related to the railroad ticket clerk, but this must be a mistake having its origin in the fact that there are certain traits and atrocities of character common to both. The hotel clerk has no relations. Not one man in a thousand can remember ever having seen a hotel clerk's father or uncle. If we were asked why this is so, we could no more account for it than we could for the fact that the cuckoo does not suckle her own young.

The night clerk is not so gorgeous or inclement as the day clerk. He wears a smaller finger-ring and a larger boot. His duties are not so onerous as are those of the day clerk: He sleeps in a chair near the stove, or reads Lakeside Library novels all night, and his most important duty is to wake up and speed the parting guest who goes off on the morning train.

24 The hotel clerk has much to try him, and perhaps we would find many excuses for what we consider his exasperating peculiarities, if we stood on his side of the register, and had the experience of how it feels to be a target for the grumbling, the fault-finding, and the interrogatories of the average traveler who lives on cornbread and bacon at home, but howls loud and long because he does not get turtle-soup and four kinds of pie three times a day when he stops at a hotel.

THE EARLY BIRD

Somebody is going to mutilate Gilhooly with a club yet, if he is not careful. A few nights ago he was returning home from an oyster supper at about two o'clock in the morning. He was full of mischief and other intoxicating beverages. Stopping at a drug store on Austin avenue, he rang the night bell, and was admitted by the clerk, who thought it must be a case of great urgency.

"Give me dimesh worth of toilet shoap."

"Do you mean to say that you disturb me at this hour of the morning to sell you a piece of soap, for which there is no immediate necessity?"

"Jesh so, no 'mediate neshessity," replied Gilhooly, putting a dime on the counter. "No 'mediate neshessity at all. Jesh keep it for me. I'll jesh drop in tomorrer and get it when I goesh home to dinner. Goodbye, Mishter apop—apotheypop, good-bye, Mishter shopopecary."

The drug clerk kicked him twice as he withdrew.

THE COWBOY

Have you seen the prairie Centuar,
Of the "Kavey-yard" the center,
Of his horse and cows the mentor—
As it were?

With a firm seat in the saddle,
He will ride what he can straddle,
And drink whiskey like his dad will—
On a "tare."

A sombrero wide his hat is,
The crown open like a lattice,
A coat he'll hardly ev—that is—
Seldom wear.

And his blond mustache he dyes it,
'Till you could not recognize it,
And he'd varnish it and size it—
If he dare.

And this burly-headed gent, he,
Just now age one and twenty,
Spends his money free and plenty—
And he'll swear.

That ten dollars, he will lay it,
On the cards, and beat your lay-out,
If you merely try to play it—
On the square.

When sometimes he is defiant,
And his will it is not pliant,
If you pistol ain't reliant—
Have a care.

When the cowboy's life is ended,
'Cross the Styx his soul they'll send it,
For he never has depended—
On a prayer.

Although the cowboy is undoubtedly a cow-catcher, he does not travel on a railroad train when he catches cows, but on the back of a pony. The cow-catcher on the locomotive is an entirely different sort of institution, but it is just as careless about whose cattle it picks up as the cow-catcher on the pony is said to be. When the cow-catcher on wheels picks up a cow or a yearling, the railroad company has to ray three or four times its value; but when the cowboy comes across a stray maverick, it is very difficult to persuade him that it did not belong to him in the first place.

The cowboy can always be found hid under a large hat, as pictured in the portrait at the head of this article. The reason he wears a hat of this size, is because no larger ones are made. The same remark applies to his spurs, which are large enough to be mistaken for the spurs of a mountain. We do not know why the cowboy always leaves his swallow-tail coat, black stove-pipe hat and kid gloves at home when he goes out on the trail, but, perhaps, he is afraid he might stampede the herd if he undertook to head them off in that garb.

There is one toy, however, which the cowboy never leaves at home when he goes to Kansas, and that is his pistol. He uses it to celebrate the Fourth of July with, and he always celebrates the great National holiday whenever he can procure the materials to celebrate with, and he is very apt to procure them if they are on the place. The reason the cowboy celebrates the great natal day of American independence so much, is because he is overloaded with patriotism. Traveling on the road, without an almanac, the cowboy manages to forget what the day of the month is, so, to be sure, he celebrates the day whenever he gets to a town. If the cowboy were provided with almanacs, so that he could tell when to celebrate the Fourth, it would be a good idea, and perhaps assist in removing the impression that the cowboy drinks whiskey and shoots off his pistol from other than patriotic motives.

If the cowboy were to cease celebrating so much, his breath would not be as strong as it is. It is so strong, occasionally, that if he would only tie a slip knot in the end of it, he could rope and hold a steer with it. He often celebrates the glorious Fourth in a Kansas

28 town and in the middle of winter. At least he makes it so hot for everybody in the town that the citizens think, from the sultriness, that July cannot be very far off.

THE SOLEMN BORE

The solemn bore is unlike the confidential bore, in that he never winks nor punches you in the ribs; neither does he punish you with a recital of the current scandal of the neighborhood. The solemn bore's chief characteristics are dignity, a monotonous voice, and statistics. He usually carries a walking stick and abounds in large feet. He invariably suffers from some disease that has puzzled all the doctors, and that he is very proud of, although he pretends to consider it a great affliction. He never tires of describing the symptoms of the disease and his manner of applying his favorite remedy. He does everything by rule, and he boasts of it. When he undresses he folds his trousers, and lays a brick on them to prevent them from bagging at the knees. It takes him half an hour to explain the process, but he never grudges the time. One of the solemn bore's strong points is proverbs, of the "early to bed, early to rise" brand, and he believes, and reiterates his belief, that the whole human family is going rapidly down to an early grave because it will not use Graham bread for breakfast, and refrain from the use of ice water at dinner.

But it is in statistics he shines. He rolls such words and phrases as one per cent., per capita, like ratio, acreage, etc., like a sweet morsel under his tongue.

The solemn bore speaks in a slow and ponderous way and pays very little attention to what you say; 29 in fact, he prefers to do most of the talking himself. He speaks of the good old times, and compares them with these degenerate days, and he shakes his head and says he is afraid to think of what the future has in store for such a frivolous people as we have become.

The solemn bore stays with you longer than any other member of the bore family, and when he leaves, it takes you all the rest of the day to get over the impression that this is a very wicked world, and that it is coming to a Sodom-and-Gomorrah end very soon.

At a moment's notice he can give you the voting population of every State in the Union, and tell the majority that elected every governor of the State since years before he was born; and when he comes to exports and import, and gets talking of bullion, and bar iron, and breadstuffs, he is the personification of addition, subtraction, the rule of three and vulgar fractions; and that is about the time you begin to wish you had never been born.

THE TEXAS COW

Mr. Webster says that the cow is "a quadruped whose abundant milk furnishes food and profit to the farmer." Mr. W. does not give the cow as much attention as she deserves, and when he talks of abundant milk, he proves beyond all question that he is densely ignorant regarding the Texas cow.

There are several kinds of cows; for instance, there is the town cow, a very enterprising animal, that breaks into the front garden at night and crowds her stomach with valuable shrubs and costly tropical plants, and that sleeps on the sidewalk in conveniently dark places, where people can fall over her without getting out of their way.

Then there is the country cow that you see—in chromos—standing meditatively in shallow streams or pools of water with her tail furled in the shape of a letter S over her back, or being driven home in the twilight along shady lanes by barefooted boys; that same cow that, out of the picture, is always breaking into the corn fields and being chased by dogs and infuriated farmers.

And there is the cow with the crumpled horn, and the ambitious cow whose lunar feat is recorded in the ancient nursery rhyme; but more important than any of these is what might be called the literary cow—the one that, ornamented with fragments of the English alphabet, roams over the Texas prairies; she has no pedigree, and is seldom found at agricultural shows or stock exhibitions. She is built in the Tudor style of architecture, and is principally composed of lean rib roasts and soup bones attached to a wide-spreading *31* pair of horns. Her time is mostly taken up in eating grass and in trying to lose herself.

A Texas cow, when she is new, is worth from $10 to $15. She is called old after she has lived eight years, unless her enterprising owner files the wrinkles off her horns; then she can be driven to town and sold for a new cow guaranteed to give three gallons of pure milk a day.

As the Texas cow, raised on the prairie, is seldom educated up to three gallons a day, and would starve, rather than eat bran or slops, the city man finds that he, as well as the cow, has been well sold; and when his wife calls him an old fool, and says that she told him so all along, he goes · off and bribes a butcher to take the cow off his hands. The butcher kills her and advertises the remains as "choice corn fed."

There are millions of cows in Texas, and some men own more than 100,000 head of cattle. There are several cattle owners who each brand from 5,000 to 20,000 calves every year. The owner brands his calves with either the initials of his name or a combination of letters, figures and hieroglyphics, and when he sells, he puts his brand on a fresh place on the animal; this is called counter-branding. Then the new owner puts his brand, consisting of three or four two-foot letters, on a blank space. After a Texas cow has been sold five or six times, she looks as if a sum in algebra had broken out all over her.

There are two kinds of branding irons and two modes of branding: one iron is of the shape of the letter or letters forming the brand, and, being heated, is stamped on the animal's side or hip, and held there until it burns through the hair and almost through

32 the skin. The other, called a running brand, is a long piece of iron curved at the end. With this, the curved end being red hot, the person branding writes the brand much after the free and fluent style in which shipping clerks mark boxes. In the most common mode of branding, the animal is thrown down and the head held to the ground until the owner's trademark is blown in the bottle, as it were. The less common way is to drive the animal into a narrow passage called a chute, just wide enough for it to squeeze through, and while it is in this tight place it is cauterized.

After all this trouble taken by man, with a view to improve and ornament the cow, the ungrateful brute fails to show any appreciation of the kindness, and even groans and kicks when the artist applies the iron. So dissatisfied does she seem, that one would almost be compelled to believe she does not care to receive and circulate the English alphabet. There is no enterprise about a cow, anyhow, except in chewing up the family underclothing, and in the matter of lifting a garden gate off its hinges, or a milkmaid off her stool.

THE TEXAS RED ANT

There are several kinds of ants in Texas, but the red one comes most into public notice.

Like all redheaded animals, this ant is of a very irascible turn of mind. When angry, the red ant knows no bounds to its rage, and respects no person or part of a person. It shows its temper most at picnics, but it has been even known to bite a good little boy on his way to Sunday school. Except, perhaps, the wasp, the red ant is the least amiable of insects.

There are a great many different sizes of ants, assorted as if manufactured to suit the different tastes of different people; but the sting of the smallest of them is large enough to satisfy the most captious; at

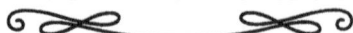

34 least, the party who gets stung is usually willing, in the heat of the moment, to swear that it is as large as a ten-penny nail. The most common and unpopular kind of an ant is an unhappy medium between extremes. Although he does not live and have his nest in the busy haunts of men, he is disposed to be rather familiar at times. To begin at the front end of the ant, he has two feelers growing out of the bumps of mirthfulness on his large, full forehead. These feelers are used in shaking hands with other ants.

Like the man who has his quarrel just, the red ant is doubly armed, having for a mouth a pair of pincers that will bite off the corner of an iron safe. At the southern end of him Providence has provided him with a javelin not unlike the hip-pocket weapon of the wasp, and which he uses with both celerity and liberality when occasion offers. At barbecues and picnics, when man tramples on the rights and property—the hearths and homes of the ant, that insect is very apt to take part in a joint discussion; and usually a delegation of ants, with a reprehensible lack of modesty, will climb upward under the clothing of the seeker after rural joys, and seizing a piece of him in their unmerciful jaws, shake and tug at it as the boarder does in his efforts to masticate the spring chicken of the city boardinghouse.

Having securely anchored his head, the ant humps himself, like unto an irate cat on a fence, and then drives several yards of envenomed sting into the leg of the unsuspecting excursionist, who, for a moment afterward, is undecided whether he should climb a tree or take off his clothes and go in swimming. He usually compromises by dancing the Can-can and using language not intended for publication, but merely given as a guarantee of good faith.

The way a single red ant can make a lazy man get up and move around is truly wonderful. Solomon must 35 have had such a scene in his mind when he told the sluggard to go to the ant.

The ant does not work during the winter months, but remains at home and sits by the fire all day telling lies about the peculiar winters they used to have when he first came to Texas. It was for a long time a disputed point as to whether ants worked at night, until a scientist from Boston received light and other experience on the subject, when he was visiting Austin last year for the benefit of his health. He procured the services of the hotel clerk to aid him in his researches. Armed with a walking-cane and accompanied by a lantern, they went out one night and found an ant hill. The scientist brought an eye-glass to bear on the ant hill at short range, while the genial hotel clerk stirred up the ants' nest with the cane. Soon the doubts of the scientist as to the late working hours of the ant were removed. When he returned to his room, upward of twenty healthy specimens of an ant, with a Latin name a yard long, were removed from his scientific anatomy with a pair of tongs.

HE HAD JUST HAD ONE

"Don't you want a glass?" asked the man who rents operate glasses at the Austin opera house, of a country man from Onion Creek.

"Don't care if I do take a glass after the show is over, but ain't thirsty now. Just had one."

POWER OF THE PRESS
IN TEXAS

HOW A TEXAS EDITOR TRAVELED
ON A RAILROAD PASS

The night train on the Santa Fe road had just arrived at Milano Junction, and the passengers were changing cars. The International and Great Northern train was waiting, and the passengers by the Santa Fe were climbing on board, and among them was a shabbily dressed young man wearing a black slouch hat, and a mustache to match. The latter was dyed, however. It was four o'clock in the morning, and the proceedings were carried on by colored lanterns, that gave some people the blues and made others look green. The young man referred to was about to climb up into the car, when the brakeman laid an official hand on his arm, and asked him to show his ticket.

"Didn't you never get to see a ticket before? Do you think I am traveling around over the country hunting up lantern-jawed brakesmen to show them tickets? Why don't you go to the ticket office and ask the ticket agent to let you look at a ticket if you want to see one so badly? Just mention my name to him and he'll give you a handful. Do you think I am the advance agent of a variety show, or a circus, or a female minstrel troupe, that you have to bore me for a ticket? Why don't you save up your wages and buy tickets if you want to amuse yourself? Why don't you ask Jay Gould to furnish you with circus tickets? He can afford it; I can't."

There was a crowd trying to push into the car, and in the confusion that particular tourist was lost sight of. How he ever got into the car is a profound mystery, but very likely he crawled under the train and got in from the opposite side. At any rate, it is a matter of history that when the train pulled out of Milano Junction for Austin, that very same young man who had such a flow of language was on board. He was not only on board, but as fast asleep as if he had traveled all night in that very car. Most of the other passengers were asleep in various picturesque attitudes, but none of them seemed to sleep quite so soundly as the man who had not got into the sheepfold through the door, but had climbed over some other way. He had evidently nothing on his mind to worry him. He looked as if even an invitation to take a drink might not have aroused him.

Presently the conductor came along. He was a tall, rawboned man, with a big nose and a still bigger mustache. He wore a green lantern and a very solemn expression of countenance. He went through the car hunting up the guilty parties who had got into the car at Milano, intending to furnish them with an opportunity to contribute a trifle each to assist the company in extending their line to the Rio Grande. Presently he came to the sleeper. He held up the lantern and gazed with a perplexed look on the green but matured cheek of the dreamer. Then the conductor smiled a sardonic, frozen smile that would have made a dead man feel uneasy, and reaching over, he shook the slumberer, and said, in a hoarse voice:

"TICKET!"

But the Bohemian, for such he was, dreamed on. At last he rubbed his eyes and asked if this was Austin.

The conductor once more brought up the ticket ques-
38 tion. "Ticket! Why, I have got a pass. I showed it to
you two hours ago. Don't worry me," and the drowsy
man dozed off again and was fast asleep in less than a
minute, but the grim-visaged conductor reached over
and shook him as a terrier does a rat. That woke him
up, but he did not wake up in good humor.

"This is the goll darndest road in Texas, and it ought
to be closed out. A gentleman can't have a minute's
rest. What in the world did you shake me for? Do
you suppose that I have been taking laudanum by
mistake, and have to be shook up and walked about
by the arm? Is that what the railroad company pays
you ten dollars a month for, or are you just hintin'
you want me to treat you? If you want a drink why
don't you come out like a man and say so? Wait—till—
we—get—to—Austin—and I'll—set—'em-up," and he
was about to doze off once more, when the conductor
bawled:

"LEMME SEE YOUR PASS!"

He woke up with a jerk. He looked in his pocket. It
was gone. He took off his hat and looked in it. No
pass. He looked under the seat, and then out of the
window at the trees which were visible by the early
light, to see if his pass was there. Then he looked sus-
piciously at the passengers, and finally he said to the
conductor:

"You never gave me back that pass."

"Never saw you or your pass before. What's your
name?" and the conductor took out a book, and began
to study.

"Let me hold your lantern, colonel," said the representative of the press, trying to look over the list of
names in the book.

"Bill Snort, editor and proprietor of the Crosby county *Clarion and Farmer's Vindicator*, a weekly journal 39
devoted to the prosperity of Texas, and the advance-
ment of the great railroad interests of the State. The
Clarion and Farmer's Vindicator is also a great religious journal."

"No pass was ever issued to any such person."

Bill Snort laughed scornfully, and said, "I reckon
that's all you know about Jay Gould. I expect you will
make a very good conductor in time, but you ain't the
kind of a man he is going to entrust with his business
plans. Jay don't keep you posted. Just you write him a
line, and ask if he didn't give William B. Snort a pass
for valuable consideration."

"Three dollars and six bits is the fare to Austin."

"Cash?"

"Cash down, quick, or I'll bounce you off at the next
station we come to."

"If you are going to put me off, I want you to put
me right back where you got me. You can either go
back to Milano right now, or I'll stay on the train and
come back with you tomorrow from Austin. Just suit
yourself. It's not my funeral. Where, Mister, can I tap
Jay Gould by wire ? "

The impudence of Bill rather amused the grim-look-
ing conductor, while it absolutely convulsed even the
passengers who were fast asleep.

"I'll tell you what," said Bill, "never mind the money. I'll give you a puff in the *Clarion*. I'll say what a
gentlemanly conductor you are, and how passengers
travel back and forward over the road just for the
fun of talking to you, and I'll send Jay a marked copy.
Perhaps he will promote you, and take you into the
firm and give you a railroad of your own."

The conductor said 'he was about tired of that mon-

keying, and to hand out the money.

40   "I'd just as lief as not pay the money, only I know Jay will get on his ear and make some railroad changes if he hears of it, and he will be mighty apt to hear of it. I only want to give you a chance to save yourself. If Gould fires you out, the only railroad in Texas that will employ you will be some street railroad, and you won't have no chance to steal a blamed cent, for conductors are not allowed to handle the fare at all in street cars. That would about break you up."

"If you put anything about me in your blamed paper, the coroner will think a freight train ran over you length-ways. I'll punch your head for you. Now you hand out that three dollars and six bits, or out you go!"

Seeing that the conductor meant business, Mr. Snort reached down in his clothes and brought out a roll of greenbacks, remarking, "Some smart people think editors never have any money. Here is a five-dollar bill. I would have paid long ago, only I sorter liked your looks, and I didn't want you and Jay to lock horns, for fear you might hurt him, he being an intimate friend of mine. He has a big family depending on him for their daily bread, and I hate to see anything happen them. Take your money, I reckon you'll be buying yourself some fresh clothes pretty soon."

The conductor was too mad to talk, so he passed on, and the man who wields the Archimedean lever in Crosby County, put his feet up on the seat in front, and began to converse with the other passengers.

"Darn a State, anyhow, where the press has no influence. No wonder it don't boom. Three dollars and six bits gone to swell up that conductor with whiskey and crackers. But it's not going to come out of my pocket. Somebody will have to bleed for this. There is one comfort about it. You all saw me pay my way. The Crosby County *Clarion* is the only paper in the State 41 that is independent of railroad monopolies. We fight to the bitter end, and the people know it. I have paid my fare, and nobody in this car will sneer at me, and take me for a member of the legislature. That's worth a thousand dollars to a gentleman of refinement like myself."

He paused to catch his breath, and then placing his finger on the breast of a drummer, who was speechless with admiration at the cheek of the Texas journalist, he asked, "Isn't that a flask?" The drummer held it out to him. After taking a pull, he put it in his own side pocket, and looking around, asked, "Ain't we going to smoke? Ain't any of us going to pass around the cigars? What sort of a crowd is this, anyhow, that tries to bulldoze the press?"

Nobody responded, so he reached in his own vest pocket, and produced the stump of a cigar. He subsided until the transfer agent asked him if he had any baggage.

"Baggage? Why, of course, I've got baggage. Do I look like an irresponsible person? Why don't you ask me if I have any clothes on. Can't you see for yourself that I am a whole clothing store? I have so much baggage that there was no room for it in the baggage car, so I had to charter a freight train. Call for the bill of lading at the hotel."

When we last saw him he was in a grocer's delivery wagon on his way to call on the Governor.

A MODEL VISITOR

A few days ago, Mr. Lawler of Williamson County, paid the sanctum of *Texas Siftings* a friendly visit. It is not unusual for us to be thus honored. Almost every day some polite gentleman calls in to see us with a bill to collect or some other testimonial of regard. Mr. Lawler, however, came on a different mission. We desire to call attention to him. We desire other visitors, and those who expect to become visitors, to model on him, for he is the kind of an intruder we want to see frequently. Such disturbers as Mr. Lawler interrupt us very agreeably. For the information of all who visit newspaper offices, we will first tell what he did not do.

He did not put his feet upon the table and tamper with the exchanges. He did not give us a mile and a half of advice how to make the paper popular with the masses. This alone made us look on him in the light *43* of a sainted angel. He did not startle us with a new joke that he claimed to have originated last week, but which we remembered to have heard in a circus thirty years ago. Neither did Mr. Lawler tell us anything about Sam Houston and the early history of Texas, or about his having shot a deer, away back in 1840, on the spot where the capitol now stands. The failure of Major Lawler to commit any of these outrages impels us to put him in nomination fol governor, which we hereby do.

And now we propose to state precisely just what Col. Lawler did.

The first thing this noble-hearted friend did was to go away at the expiration of ten minutes after he entered the office. As soon as he entered he drew out two dollars, did this nature's nobleman, this high-toned Southern gentleman, Gen. Lawler, and renewed his subscription which had not yet expired, remarking that *Siftings* was the very best paper in Texas. Yes, that's just what this heaven-born old Texan, Gen Lawler, said. Then he produced a bottle from a basket, and proceeded to cheer up the Sifters with the contents, remarking once more that he was an admirer of the paper, which deserved to be framed in gold. The contents of the bottle was not the vile stuff called "home-made mustang wine," with which old grangers disorganize the internal economy of inexperienced journalists, but was ice cold beer.

After this seraphic old hero, Gen. Lawler, had drunk a glass to the prosperity of *Texas Siftings*, amid the blushes of the editors, he said he would not think of occupying more of our valuable time, and bade us farewell, but not before he had produced a second

44 bottle, which he forced on us, with an injunction to drink it as soon as we got lonesome or thirsty, both of which mental and bodily sensations we began to experience as soon as our generous friend was outside the door, and not likely to return to get any of it—the beer, we mean.

Now visitors know how we are to be conciliated. It should be mentioned, however, that there is no intention of limiting their enthusiasm. If instead of two bottles of beer Gen. Lawler had brought two kegs, that would not have diminished our high regard for him. If he had brought in a few boxes of cigars, even that would not have lessened our admiration for his many good qualities of heart and head.

Gen. Lawler's past life has been blameless as far as we know, except that he owned up to being personally intimate with Nat Q. Henderson, of the Georgetown *Record*, but those who know Nat will readily understand how a man who carries bottled beer about with him could hardly help being rather intimate with him so long as the beer lasted.

RECKLESS LOCAL REPORTER

The yearning of Americans after titles has often been very properly ridiculed. If a man has never been on the bench since he was a school boy, unless it was on the mourner's bench in the recorder's court for being drunk and disorderly, he is in more danger than almost anybody else of being called "judge." If a man has been gifted with sufficient strategic ability to keep out of the late attempt to destroy the United States government, that man is liable to go through 45 life with "colonel" or "major" in front of his name. The best way would be to make the laws apply to everybody who forges complimentary titles. For this nonsense the press is largely responsible. There is a disposition on the part of local reporters to write down every man "general" or "colonel" who happens to brighten up the reportorial horizon with a cheap cigar or a bottle of sour wine. The readers take their cue from the newspaper, and the consequence is that when men are sentenced to the penitentiary or arrested for taking clothes off a line, the judge and the constable address them as "general," "judge," "colonel," or whatever may be the stigma that attaches to their names.

The Texas papers, in particular, have another bad habit they might advantageously shuffle off. If a little one horse corner grocer finds favor in the eyes of the faber-pusher he is denounced through the press as a merchant prince. It is more than probable that reporters who are so liberal in conferring princely titles have a very much muddled-up idea as to what kind of coffee mill a prince really is. A real prince never slaps a reporter on the back and calls him Bob, or Dick, or whatever other name his sponsors in baptism have bestowed upon him. A *bona fide* prince never sits in his shirt sleeves in front of his store and squirts tobacco juice through his front teeth. A real prince is always dressed in a most gorgeous military uniform, with a big silver star as big as a saucer on his breast, to let people know that he is the prince, and no mistake. A prince is always calm, reserved, dignified, and surrounded by a glittering staff. If a newspaper man were to run up to that kind of a prince and ask him

for a pound of cheese and crackers on ninety days'
46 credit, half-a-dozen dukes, counts, earls, and like small
fry would telephone for a policeman to show the journalist the road to the lunatic asylum. There is no such
thing as a merchant prince.

The Texas journalist also persists in calling every
Stockman who brands all the calves in his neighborhood a cattle king. No real king ever wore an old
slouch hat and lived on cornbread and coffee. The real
king sits upon a glittering throne, such as you see
in circus processions, holding a golden sceptre like a
policeman's club, in his hand, and a royal crown on his
head. The king of diamonds is a pretty fair likeness
of a highborn sovereign. Now, what is there about an
alleged cattle potentate that justifies the reporter in
dubbing him with the title of king?

But the most serious charge we have to make
against the average reporter is the kind of marriage
notice that is sprung on the unfortunate couple by
the local reporter. It is an undeniable fact that what
are called society people, like the angels in Heaven,
are neither married nor given in marriage. There is
a great deal of buggy riding but comparatively little pushing about of baby carriages. There is no end
to pie-nicking, moonlight rambles, but very few brid-
al tours among fashionable people. There is a great
deal of skirmishing along the line, but no regular en-
gagement. And all this hesitancy is occasioned by the
dread of a cheerful send-off by the local reporter.

We once knew a local reporter, in a Texas city,
who materially reduced the census by his flattering
marriage notices. He was not satisfied with the usual twaddle about " the fair and lovely bride," "the
noble-looking groom," and "the high contracting
parties," but he would invariably wind up the notice

with a few verses of poetry. It did not make a particle of difference to him what kind of poetry it was. He **47** had a dictionary of poetical quotations at hand, and would chop off a piece at random. Occasionally it fitted, but sometimes the verse reminded one of Sancho Panza's proverbs dragged in backward by the tail. On the occasion of the nuptial of a well-known doctor, he wound up the notice with Longfellow's familiar verse beginning:

"There is a reaper, whose name is Death."

The doctor came very near gathering in that local reporter. On another occasion, where a young man, who had been very fast, reformed and got married, the local reporter seized his dictionary of classical quotations and made him happy with the verse from Gray's Elegy in a Country Church Yard, beginning:

"No further seek his frailties to disclose."

Such marriage notices kept people from adorning their necks with the marriage yoke. It was useless to attempt to modify his zeal. Men about to get married would beg him with tears in their eyes to treat them with silent contempt, but as soon as the wine and cake began to tell on his reportorial stomach, in one wild outburst of gratitude, he would perpetrate half a column of inspired idiocy. Occasionally some desperate man would fail to send the usual cake and wine, and then was startled by reading that the bride's mother was a servant girl but rose to her present position by industry and saving, and that the bridegroom's father is the only one of four brothers who escaped the penitentiary.

There can be no doubt but that the recklessness with which the newspaper man writes up marriage notices has much to do with the unwillingness of

fashionable young men and maidens to get married.
48 Some people say that the real cause is the inability
of the fashionable young wife to get along with an
expensive colored cook lady, a colored wash lady and
perhaps a nurse lady, not to speak of her "ma" We
nearly overlooked that venerable obstacle. Then, too,
they say fashionable hats, and cotton, and paint, cost
like the very mischief. These depressing influences
may have some effect in discouraging marriages, but
the real Jonah is the reckless local reporter.

THE SIFTERS SEEK
RELAXATION & GO
GUNNING FOR QUAIL

We have a friend who lives in the country a few miles from Austin. He is a farmer—one of those kinds of agriculturalists who earn their bread by the sweat of the hired man's brow. His horny hands are not the result of intimate association with a hoe, but are acquired by hauling big fish out of creek, and carry home game bags full of snipe and partridge and ducks. He comes in to see us once in a while and tells us fish stories, and tries to discourage us from our task of moulding public opinion by describing the pleasures of rural life; the delights of raising cotton on the uplands and cane among the game birds in the valleys; the joyful glee of farming with negro renters "on the shares," and the unalloyed felicity and hilarity of lying on one's back in the sylvan shades of Onion creek and drinking buttermilk.

This friend of ours—for convenience sake, we will call him Tiff Johnson, because that is his name—has an accomplice in the person of a wicked brother, who aids and abets him in his unholy practice of making poor city editors dissatisfied with their lot, and causing them to yearn for the tranquility of the rural precincts where newspaper exchanges cease from troubling and the weary editor may have rest. He dropped in a few days ago, and, after telling us about something that happened to a bow that was never unbent, suggested that we needed a day's rest, and invited us to go out to his place and shoot quail. We intimated that we did not think that prancing over corn rows all day would be what might be called a rest. He said that we would not need to go into the corn fields at all, that usually quail stayed in corn fields, but that this year they were so plenty that the corn fields would not hold them, and you could see them everywhere oozing out of the cracks in the ·fences and find them all over the prairies. On this

assurance we consented to spend the next day (last
50 Friday) unbending ourselves and slaughtering quail.

To this end we rented two breech-loading guns, and
fifty rounds of deadly cartridges for each gun.

The Sifter who some eighteen years ago assist-
ed in discouraging the Union army, by guarding a
camp-fire down at Indianola, was supposed to be an
excellent shot—at least he had acquired that reputation from the stories he told of marching around in
gore during the war.

The other Sifter, who was once an Irishman by
profession, never had had any practice in shooting,
except at landlords, and did not have much confidence
in his skill in shooting on the wing; but was sure that
he could make a line shot on a quail, if he could get
him on the ground and creep up on him from behind a
fence. However, we were both enthusiastic, and went
to bed full of determination to let no guilty creature,
with feathers on it, escape. The writer had a dreadful
dream. He dreamed that he was surrounded by a covey of fierce quail. They were forming a circle around
him. He was unable to move hand or foot. He saw in
his dream his faithful gun lift up one paw, as if there
was a thorn in it, while his tail became as rigid and
pointed as the finger of scorn. At this critical moment, when hope seemed dead and escape impossible,
the other Sifter appeared on the scene, and bringing
his double-barreled dog to his shoulder, he fired. Just
then the writer awoke, and found his wife slamming
him on the ear, trying to awaken him that he might
start early on his errand of slaughter.

The sun was just peering above the eastern horizon, and the morning dew would have been on the
grass-only that dew does not fall in Western Texas—
as we started. After a drive of some six miles, we met

our friends—the Johnson brothers—and proceeded to drive about five miles farther over the prairie before we were detected by a single quail. At this point we got out of the buggy and partook of some refreshments, and proceeded on foot about two miles, when our feet became sore. We were about to inquire of our country friends if this wasn't an off day with quails, when—whir—whirr—whirrr! a dozen birds flew up. Bang—bang—bang! The birds that we shoot at do not fall fluttering to the ground. They vanish like a schooner of beer in the presence of the editor of the Houston *Age*. We hear the country fellows laugh. They have bagged three birds.

One of us city fellows managed to hit something. It was the right shoulder, and it was quite black next day. A tramp of a mile, and we discover some more birds, and two entirely new blisters on each of our heels. We get one of these birds, and feel satisfied that we would have got them all, but for the unnecessary precipitancy with which they left the deadly neighborhood.

At this point we take some more refreshments and a rest. Then we walk some more. We wonder why the birds do not alight on the trees or on a fence. What are trees and fences for, anyhow? We surprise a jack-rabbit, and scare him badly by planting lead in the landscape all around him. We proceed in this manner for several hours, getting a few birds, intimidating vast numbers, and getting more blisters on our feet.

Then we concluded that we had unbended ourselves sufficiently, and had had enough rest for one day. Our country friends had a large bag full of birds. We had seven quail, one lark, and a fly-up-the-creek. We had been laboring under the delusion that it was cheap-

52 er to go out and shoot quails than to buy them at a restaurant.

We are not of that opinion now, as will be shown, with ghastly distinctness, in the following statement:

LIABILITIES.

To 100 cartridges, No. 10.	$3.50
To beer and other refreshments	$3.00
To pocket knife broken in opening beer bottle	.50
Arnica for shoulder	.25

ASSETS.

By 5 cartridges on hand.	17 ½
By 7 quails, market price	70
By 1 lark, market price	05
By 1 fly-up-the-creek, no value	6 32½
	$7.25

It will be seen that our liabilities exceed our assets by $6.32½, or, in other words, our nine birds cost us an average of about eighty cents each, without taking into consideration the wear and tear of the guns and our heels.

We propose to work right along now, without relaxation in the quail shooting line, for the next seventy-five years.

A tramp who was stealing a ride on a freight train near San Antonio, was recently killed by a railroad accident. This should be a· solemn warning to tramps never to steal a ride. Let the tramp tear his clothes, punch a hole in his hat, paint his nose red, and then apply to the president of the road for a free pass as a member of the press. A tramp has no earthly excuse to steal a ride.

SAN ANTONIO MEXICANS

Since the fall of the Alamo there has been a slow and gradual change in the aspect of the city of San Antonio; the enterprise and civilization of the American taking the place of the apathy, ignorance and shiftlessness of the Mexicans.

The old and new are brought together in violent contrast in San Antonio. Here the Mexican jacal, with its thatched roof and adobe walls; across the street the palatial residence of an American or German resident, with its surroundings of flowers and fountains. Now a narrow and crooked street is intersected by a broad avenue, lined with trees, where we see the carriage of the broadcloth-covered American passing the ragged Mexican's donkey-cart, of a pattern used 200 years ago. Farther on we see a cockpit on the same block with a Methodist church, while we hear the creak of

the huge Mexican carretas mingling with the rattle
54 of the railroad cars.

The San Antonio river flows through the city. A range of hills, with a gradual elevation of 200 feet, almost surround the valley in which San Antonio is situated. The altitude of San Antonio above the level of the Gulf of Mexico is 687 feet; average temperature, spring, 69.90; summer, 83.50; autumn, 68.90; and winter, 52.90 degrees.

The city has now a population of about 22,000. Of this number six thousand are Mexicans. The balance includes representatives of almost every nation on earth.

The Mexican element in the population is what makes San Antonio differ so much from every other city in the United States. The average Mexican is a mixture of Spaniard, Indian and negro. There is nothing thoroughbred about him; and, even if he were washed, he would have but little to boast of over the Indian. It may be conceded that he is more of a success in raising a crop of small-pox; but, outside of that, he possesses no virtue nor personal charm that the Indian has not. The Mexicans are, as a class, probably the poorest citizens in the United States. The Mexican who squanders twenty-five cents a day on the support of his family and dogs, is looked upon as a man in easy circumstances, and of prodigal habits.

Upon arriving at San Antonio, one of the first things the tourist from the north wants to see is a Mexican "jackal." That, at least, is what he asks for. He has read about "the dark-eyed daughters of old Castile," sitting at the door of the Mexican jacal. A jacal is a Mexican hut; (the word is pronounced hackal.) Nine-tenths of the houses in the valley of the Rio Grande are jacals. A jacal is a den hardly fit for a jackal to

live in. It consists of one room, 12x12, and is construct- 55
ed by driving a number of posts into the ground, very
slowly—that is, it takes a Mexican about half a day
to plant one post, and the other half of the day to be
on the ground and look at it from different directions
to see if it is set in straight. The posts are planted
close together, and the space between is daubed with
mud. The roof is made with cane, thatched with tule.
There is an opening in the side of the jacal, used for
the entrance and exit of the inhabitants. A blanket
with enough holes in it to justify it being washed by
the dozen, usurps the place of a door. The inside walls
are adorned with cheap and highly-colored pictures
of saints with blue legs and purple hair. These saints
bear a startling resemblance, in facial expression
and general anatomical construction, to those high
personages, the king and jack of diamonds. There is
no attempt at gorgeousness in the way of furniture.
A couple of benches and a few goat skins comprise
the parlor set. The library, dining-room, parlor, stable,
kitchen, picture-gallery and sleeping apartments are
all in one room on the ground floor. When the owner is
influential and opulent, a goat pen may be discovered
in the neighborhood, and a few lean donkeys browse
around in the adjacent chaparral.

FIRE CRANKS

There are a number of stereotyped characters
who attend all fires. When you get up in night,
put your socks on wrong side out, rush down
town with one suspender trailing on the ground,
and arrive at the fire in a half dressed and breath-

less condition, you find these characters already on
the ground, and—as Artemus Ward said about the
stars in Heaven—"up to their usual doin's." There is
for instance the hoarse-voiced man who acts as if the
whole conflagration was under his personal super-
vision, and who stands on an ash barrel in the alley,
wildly gesticulating, and howling suggestions to the
chief of the fire department. He usually gets knocked
down by a ladder, or has the hose turned on him by
accident; then, when he gets all the muddy water out
of his mouth and ears, he goes off to the other side
of the street, looks on at a safe distance, and has a
great deal to say about the inefficiency of volunteer
fire departments.

An equally dangerous and absurd character is the
man with the axe. He is always early at a fire; accompanied by a new axe. No one knows where he got
the axe and no one ever sees him carrying it back to
where he got it, but, while he is on the ground, he
makes things lively. He is a perfect "besom of destruction." He batters in doors, hacks the fence in a vain
effort to cut it away to make room for the engine,
and, in his wild desire to save property, he demolishes
everything that an axe will make an impression on.
This fiend, who is too weak to do any manual labor,
and who lets his wife chop all the firewood at home,
will create havoc and desolation for two blocks around
a fire, and he has even been known, when everything,
including the lightning rod, and the pumps, was cut
down, to tum in and hew to pieces the shade trees In
the next lot to keep the fire from spreading.

Then there is the man who has an inordinate craving for a ladder. His inmost soul is stirred with a
yearning for a step ladder? In tones swelling with
pathos, profanity, and excitement, he shouts: "Have

any of you got a ladder? My Heaven! will none of you give me a ladder?" as if a twenty-four foot ladder was something that—like a six-shooter, or a charm to prevent rheumatism—everyone carried in his pocket. When he can't get a ladder, he tries to climb up the water-spout, that he may, at the risk of his life, break open some of the second story windows, let the air in, and give the fire a chance. In contrast with this last vigorous character, is the helpless man who goes about wringing his hands or carrying an empty bucket, getting in everybody's way and wondering if the building was insured. He gets tripped up by the hose and knocked about generally. He wants to stop the foreman of the fire department and ask him how the fire originated, and if he thinks there is any chance of it spreading, but the foreman has only time to address some bad words to him.

Very prominent in the crowd at every fire is the man who was the first to see it—there are usually about forty of him. He tells how—and he is very particular regarding details—he was standing talking to a friend, on the sidewalk about two blocks away, when he noticed a small quantity of smoke oozing, etc., etc., but everyone knows him well, having suffered from his egotistical narratives, and we will, therefore, dismiss him along with the man who has the defective flue theory regarding the origin of the fire, and the other man with the incendiary theory.

THE PELON DOG

The Mexicans call him *pelon*. The Americans refer to him as the no-hair dog; while the stranger from the north, who sees him for the first time, calls him a cast-iron dog, for that is what he looks like at first glance. Although not particularly intelligent, the no-hair dog is susceptible of a high polish, for his hairless hide shines in the sun as if it had recently been touched with stove-polish. His body is about the size, and somewhat of the shape, of a watermelon-that is, of one of those small watermelons that is about the size of a *pelon* dog. He differs, however from the melon in that his tail is adorned with a tuft of blonde hair, which is never the case with the watermelon. He wears a tuft of hair—another tuft, of course, not the same one—on his head, which gives him a very striking appearance.

The *pelon* dog is found in Austin, in San Antonio, and in tamales, the latter being a Mexican dish, the ingredients of which are as uncertain as those of hash. The *pelon* is a descendant of the Barbary dog. He is of a purple-blue color, has bandy legs, and is always fat. His fatness is the result of an advantage he has over all other dogs, he being as bald (with the exception of the two tufts afore mentioned) as the inside of a goose. He is not troubled, as other curs are, by detachments of flees scouting over him, and therefore does not keep himself thin with the exercise of scratching his left ear with his right hind leg. Strangers from the East, who never saw any of these bandy-legged absurdities until they came to Austin or San Antonio, are puzzled considerably when they see the naked dog for the first time. A Chicago man, just arrived in

Austin, asked the baggage man at the depot, what was "the matter with that dog?" The baggage man 59 was busy, and replied, after the pleasant, laconic manner of baggage men when they are busy: "Coal-oil lamp explosion." The Chicago man was surprised, as he walked up town, to see two or three dogs on every block with the hair apparently all singed off them. Meeting the baggage man at the hotel door, he remarked: "Say, mister, didn't-didn't the coal-oil lamp explode in a dog-factory?"

The pelon dog is a great favorite with the Mexicans in Texas. Every Mexican family owns from one to half-dozen of them, according to their means. The poorer the family, the greater number of dogs they can afford to support. It does not cost much to keep a covey of no-hair dogs, except during the month of July. Then the proprietors of the dogs are expected to come forward and pay a dollar apiece license on each and every dog, no matter whether it has hair on its back or not. Paying out that much actual cash is calculated to put a Mexican family, with six or seven dogs, back about ten years in their finances. Many of the families find it cheaper to take their *pelon* dogs and move out into the country, and only move back when the dog-catching season is over, and the dog-catchers have quit going the rounds. Other families that do not own a watermelon ranch in the country, stay at home, and tie their dogs up under their beds where the dog-catchers can't scoop them. The consequence is that the *pelon* dogs howl all night, so that strangers at the hotels can't get a wink of sleep, which injures the prosperity of the town. If it were not for these howling dogs, San Antonio, where the *pelon* dog is epidemic the whole year, would have three or four more railroads than she has.

WEBSTER BORROWS A DOLLAR

"Sam, can yer lend me a dollar that yer has no use fur?" said Jim Webster to Sam Johnsing, whom he met opposite Graham's Drug Store.

"Certaingly, Jim, I'se pleased to 'comodate yer," said Sam, handing Jim a dollar. ,

Jim was so surprised at his luck, that he bit the coin, to see if he was awake, or merely dreaming, and in doing so discovered that it was made of lead.

"This yere is a counterfeit, Sam. I didn't think you would do me that way."

"I know it's counterfeit, Jim; yer asked me fur one I had no use fur, an' I give it to yer. I'm always 'commodatin' to my friends."

BILL SNORT'S
LEGAL EXPERIENCE

We were not at all astounded a few days ago to see Bill Snort, of the Crosby County *Clarion and Farmers' Vindicator*, stroll in. After we had taken him to a saloon, and afforded him an opportunity to moisten the inner man, he was led back to the sanctum, and urged to draw up to the fire and make himself comfortable. We have some cigars at the office, which have been thrust upon us by candidates during the recent local elections. They are the sort generally used by candidates in consolidating the floating vote, and were given us inadvertently, owing to the candidate being too tight to discriminate. When a man, who is not used to that kind of cigar (two for a nickel), seeks to soothe himself with

one of them, after a few whiffs he feels a yearning
62 to get out quickly into the open air, where he can
lie down and die. Not wishing to take up much of
Bill Snort's time, by talking to him, we considerately
presented him with one of these cigars. The result
was not satisfactory to us. Instead of getting up and
seeking fresh air, he said it was the best cigar he had
smoked since the meeting of the Press Convention at
Houston.

"Well, Bill," asked one of the Sifters, "what brings
you to Austin? Now own up that your presence at
the Capital has a political significance. Col. H.B. Andrews, of San Antonio, is in town just now, and when
Gov. Roberts, Bill Snort, of the Crosby County Clarion
and Farmers' Vindicator, and Harry Andrews are in
perihelion, it means that there is plotting against the
whites. That kind of a brilliant concatenation must
mean something extraordinary."

"I didn't know Col. Andrews was in Austin. He will
be glad to know that I am here, for he is anxious to
consult with me on a matter of great importance to
his road. My pass is about run out."

There was a pause. Bill continued to enjoy that vile
cigar that was bad enough to have made a horse and
carriage sick. Finally, stretching himself out, and
blowing a cloud of smoke at the ceiling, he said, "I've
a great notion of telling you how I once collected a
$100 fee from a Scotchman in San Antonio, when I
was practicing law. You could write it up and make a
first-rate thing of it."

"Why, Bill, how did you come to practice law?"

Bill looked all around to make sure that he was not
overheard, and then said, in a low voice. "Yes, I blush
to say that, at one time, before I reformed and became
a journalist, I was in a fair way to become a hardened
criminal lawyer, but I was snatched, as a brand, from

the burning. Of course this is not for publication. It might injure my social status in Crosby County. I have **63** given up all the bad habits I contracted while practicing law. By the way, that's a telephone, ain't it?"

"Yes, that's what it is."

"Why the mischief, then, don't you connect with a saloon, and order up some whiskey toddies; what else are telephones for?"

From this we inferred that, if a vigorous effort were made, Bill might be induced to absorb another stimulant, and our worst fears were realized. As he stirred up the stuff, he remarked, closing one eye significantly, "As I was saying, when I quit the law I gave up all my bad habits. Sanctified Moses! What weak whiskey this is! It hasn't got as much strength in it as the Greenbackers have in the Legislature. Is this the kind of stuff you run *Texas Siftings* on? But I was going to tell you how I scooped in that fee."

"Did you have much civil practice?"

"I was a very civil lawyer outside of the court house, but inside I used to throw chairs and books at the opposing counsel, and sass the court as fluently as if I had been practicing for twenty years. A San Antonio jury has no reverence for a lawyer who doesn't stand up for his rights. I tell you that those San Antonio lawyers squander language on each other that is almost strong enough for the United States Senate."

"Look here, Bill, our paper goes to press on Friday, and it is Monday already. If you have got anything for us to write up, let us have it. We would like to hear about you collecting a fee from a Scotchman. We never before heard of such a feat being performed. Did you chloroform him with a club before you went through his pockets?"

"After the war," resumed Bill, "I practiced law in San Antonio. At first, and ever afterwards, people

hesitated about intrusting me with cases involving
64 large sums of money. My practice was principally of
a criminal nature. As in a hospital, the paupers are
all turned over for the young doctors to practice on,
so, in the Texas courts, pauper criminals are turned
over to the young lawyers. The young lawyers gain
a great deal of experience, but they never get any
actual cash. I had a large, but not lucrative, criminal practice. I don't know how many poor devils for
whom I, with some slight assistance from the State's
Attorney, got free transportation to Huntsville. Why, I
secured a sentence of **99** years for one man. He doesn't
know what a narrow escape he had from being com-
muted—I mean hung. If the other young attorney,
who was to help me, had not taken sick, we would
have hung that man sure."

"How about that Scotchman you robbed?"

"It came about in this way: Judge Devine, a leading lawyer of San Antonio, who likes to help incipient
young barristers along, was either moved to admiration at my success in securing permanent positions
for my clients at Huntsville Penitentiary, or else he
was carried away by compassion at the wrecked condition of my clothing. At any rate, he turned over a
number of cases to me, allowing me to retain any fee
I might succeed in embezzling from the client. One of
these was MacNab vs. Menger. I was for the plain-
tiff, who, during the war, had sold a barrel of soda
to Menger, who ran a soap factory. They disagreed
about the payment. Menger wanted to pay fourteen
thousand dollars in Confederate bonds, but MacNab
had a preference for $250 in actual hard cash, that
the rat couldn't gnaw. In his answer, Menger claimed
that he spoiled $2,000 worth of soap by using the
soda, and asked that MacNab be required to pay that

amount as damages; he farther claimed that he never had received any soda from MacNab, and finally, 65 that Texas being in rebellion, the contract was null and void *ab initio*. He procured the services of I. A. & G. W. Paschal, two great *ab initio* jurists."

"Whew! Are you going to give us this *ab initio* business *ad infinitum?*"

"Well, the first important step for me to take was to waylay MacNab and secure my fee. He kept a family grocery store, and I had a family and no groceries. I thought the unities would be preserved by my making a raid on that store and sacking it. He was a keen, shrewd Scotchman, and I anticipated trouble in making him understand that about $100 worth of groceries, in advance, was about what he ought to be glad to suffer."

"If you had only inflicted this yarn upon him, he would have submitted to the larceny just to get rid of you."

Bill, however, paid no attention to the interruption, but kept right on: "I found the store in charge of a green-looking young man, with blonde hair, blue eyes, and the broadest Scotch dialect ever brought to this country. He had only arrived a few weeks previously. He told me that MacNab was not in, at which I was not very much surprised, as I had just seen him in the courthouse. The green young man's name was Sandy MacGeddes, (Mr. MacNab called him "the young mon.") When I handed him my card, emblazoned with the legend: 'Bill Snort, Attorney and Counselor at Law,' he was nearly overpowered. He removed his hat, and looked scared. In the old country a counselor-at-law is a kind of a legal potentate, who has a wig and an ancestral castle, and never converses with anybody below the rank of a duke, except on business.

I Informed MacGeddes that I had been entrusted **66** with some of MacNab's legal business, and had therefore transferred my custom to his establishment; that I wanted about $100 in groceries. The young man intimated that he would feel flattered to take my order. As the proper time to make hay is while the bright orb of day hangs resplendent in the blue vault above—"

It was evident that the whiskey was stronger than Col. Snort had supposed it was. He was dropping into poetry. The Sifters gave him ten minutes to finish his rigmarole, promising him another drink and another Havana cigar, if he made the connection on time; if he didn't, his life was to pay the forfeit.

"I determined to make hay while the sun shone," resumed Bill. "I called a passing dray, and the way that I piled family supplies into it made the neighbors think the sheriff was selling out the concern. Sandy MacGeddes checked off the articles with delight, and a lead pencil. He was entranced at the big sale he was making. I was in a hurry for fear MacNab would return before the goods were out of sight, and refuse to ratify the proceedings of the convention. If he did return, he would probably undertake to unload the dray, and then there would be a disgraceful Roman-Greco wrestling match between a prominent lawyer and a local merchant prince. I did not care much for notoriety; it was groceries I was after; so I helped with my own hands to carry out the bottles, boxes of cigars, and like family supplies. In order not to lose any time, I took things as they came, and, in the hurry, actually captured a lot of wagon-grease, and a dozen monkey-wrenches, just to make up the even $100.

"On parting with Sandy MacGeddes, he said, with a bow, he knew Mr. MacNab would always regret not being present to entertain me; to which I replied that I had no doubt his employer would regret his absence, **67** and if he knew I was there, he ,would leave whatever he might be doing, and hurry down to the store in a hack to confer with me, after which I took a seat on the dray to protect the goods *in transitu*—another technical term you don't understand.

"I reckon I'll be through with my last words in time," said Bill. "You see, I came by those goods honestly. I had a conveyance drawn up—the dray, you know— by which conveyance the goods were conveyed into my possession. But the meeting between MacNab and Sandy MacGeddes was a tableau in itself. It threatened to end very much like the interview between *Macbeth* and *MacDuff*."

"Only seven minutes left, Bill, for you to address the assembled public, and then we will spring the trap and drop you, if you are not through talking."

"When MacNab entered the store, he stood still in astonishment, and in the doorway. He was surprised at the evidences of the big sale his "young mon" had made. The young man was jubilant over the large transaction. He expected that his employer would raise his wages on the spot.

" 'It canna be that ye hae made sic a braw sale, Sandy. I didna ken ye war sic a salesman,' said MacNab, as he glanced around at the depleted shelves.

" 'And why for no, uncle? Do ye think I canna mak' as big sales as ony ither bodie?' said the young man with the imported accent, who was disappointed because his uncle did not em brace him.

" 'Wha did ye sell tae, Sandy?'

" 'Tae a braw gentleman; ane o' thae counselors-at-law.'

" 'I'm thinkin' ye didna deleever the goods till he

paid ye?' said MacNab, anxiously.

68   Then Sandy explained the nature of the transaction, and MacNab, in speechless horror, gazed at the decimated array of canned goods, the devastation in the rows of bottles, the tenantless candle boxes, and the empty places that were full of fresh butter and eggs when he left the store in the morning. There was not a department that had not sustained severe losses.

" 'Ten dollars wad hae been nae sma' fee for sic a pettifogger as Bill Snort,' he groaned. 'If a puir attorney like Bill Snort can sack my store, I may expec' his partner, Judge Devine, the muckle pirate in the case, tae cart off the store, cellar an' a', and claim a lien on my homestead. Oh, Sandy, mon, this is awesome; ye hae ruined your auld uncle, but I'll hae the buccaneer up for gettin' awa' wi' a puir daft gowk just frae Scotland. I'll gang up an' indict him the noo."

" 'But, uncle, he is a counsellor-at-law, an' he—'

" 'Hoots, mon, dinna fash me wi' yer counsellors-at-law. They should hae keepit ye at hame. Ye're no' fit tae trade wi' San Antonio attorneys. Why didna ye set the doggie on the blackmailin' shoplifter?'

The old man sank into a chair.

" 'This is an unco sair day wi' me,' he said. 'I'm losin' my mind, Sandy, an' then I'll be no better off than yersel', you puir, freckless bodie. Gi'e me a mouthfu' o' that auld Scotch whusky.'

" 'The counsellor-at-law bought it all,' replied Sandy, in a sad tone.

" 'Gang awa an' tap a bottle o' Scotch ale, then, for I feel faint.'

" 'He's ta'en a' the ale, Uncle, but I charged him wi' sax bottles mair than he ta'en.'

"Just at this moment a colored man entered, and said, 'Boss, dat ar liar, Bill Snort, tole me ter kerlect

two bits for deliverin' a load of groceries for you at
his house.'

"MacNab reached back, nervously, into the barrel for
an axe-handle, but there was none there. I had already
bought out all the axe-handles, so he made a break at
the darkey with a chair, while the Ethiopian clubbed
his whip, and stood ready to strike. Sandy MacGeddes
seized a two-pound weight, and drew back to hurl it
at the drayman."

"How did the fight turn out?" exclaimed one of the
Sifters.

"Which whipped?" asked the other.

"I've nothing more to say. Time's up. You told me
you would only give me ten minutes. Time's up, and
I've got to go now. Col. Andrews, of the Sunset Route,
wants to see me about renewing my pass," and Bill
passed out, and we saw him no more.

*General Hamey, of the regular army, is
a thorough Irishman, and makes splendid
bulls. When he was in Texas, a brother
officer said to him one day: "I believe,
Harney, after you are dead, I'll write your
life." "If you do, I'll take yours as sure as
you are alive," was the perfectly serious
response.*

THE HOTEL WAITER

The hotel waiter is a man whose business it is to make you wait for your meals unless you give him half a dollar to encourage him in making a fast record. The hotel waiter, in the South, is a colored man who can make haste more slowly than any other creature on earth. Like the waiter that he carries the dishes on, he is black and polished. If you place half-a-dollar on the first-mentioned waiter, it makes an impression on the other waiter. He is called a waiter because he is supposed to wait on the guest, (the waitee), but the latter is really the waiter, because the waiter is — O, pshaw! this waiter business is getting mixed; there is too much of our expressive English language anyhow. But to resume, as the preachers say; when you come into the dining-room, the waiter acts as if he were afraid that you were going to change your mind and go to some other hotel. He beckons you, backs away from you, and wildly gesticulates toward a chair, which he seizes and swings away from the table, and then, when you reach the table, he pushes the chair at you from behind, and 71 strikes you on the inside hinge of the knee with force enough to· jar the cotton out of your ears. You have to sit down whether you desire to do so or not. As soon as the waiter has got you in the chair, he hands you the bill of fare and assumes an expression of countenance that is calculated to create the impression that he can read.

The memory of the average waiter is extraordinary. Some say that it is because, like some men's consciences, it is never used, but that is not so.

It is wonderful to see him standing solemnly and respectfully attentive behind a drummer's chair, while the hungry drummer reads off his selections, something in the following style: "Consomme of macaroni; baked red snapper with brown sauce; sugar-cured tongue; green goose with apple sauce (and don't forget the apple sauce, you son-of-a-gun); roast beef (an outside piece cut thin); fricasse rabbit, farmers' style; baked macaroni *au parmesan*; brazed pigeon *a la Jardinere* (just a very small piece of the pigeon, but bring dead oodles of the *a la Jardinere*); tripe fried in batter, with tomato sauce; onions; Lima beans; mashed potatoes; squash, and chow-chow."

It is still more wonderful to see the waiter return after an absence of forty-five minutes—during which time the drummer drinks three glasses of ice-water by way of entertaining his stomach while waiting— with an entirely different assortment of food. This is where evidences of his wonderful memory shine forth like a parlor match in a dark pantry. He remembers to forget everything ordered except, perhaps, mashed potatoes or roast beef, but that is seldom his fault, the chief cook having packed them inadvertently with

72 the rest of the goods. If you want roast beef, your best chance to get it is to order fried tripe or pig's feet, and if you want turnips and lettuce, the only safe way to get in conjunction with them is to order up all the vegetables, relishes, and entrees in the house, and then you have the satisfaction of finding that the only place to find them in town is on the bill of fare. "Just out ob dem, sah, very sorry, sah," the waiter says, as he hands you the mustard and smiles in a conciliatory way.

And that brings us to smiles. The colored waiter is all smiles. He smiles on the slightest provocation, whereas the white waiter of the North never smiles. The ordinary colored waiter sometimes becomes a head-waiter, after which he never smiles; but with his arms folded, *a la Napoleon*, on the Island of St. Helena, assumes a solemn and dignified position in the middle of the dining-room.

An old Texan veteran called in to see us yesterday, and he stated positively that he did not capture Santa Anna at the Battle of San Jacinto. As he is the first old Texan we have ever met who did not captvre Santa Anna, there is something very strange about it. We are afraid he is an awfvl liar, bvt perhaps he was only drunk. We do not wish to do him injustice.

LATEST GEOGRAPHICAL INTELLIGENCE

"Where is the island of Java situated?" asked an Austin school teacher of a small, rather forlorn-looking boy.

"I dunno, sir."

"Don't you know where coffee comes from?"

"Yes, sir, we borrows it ready parched from the next door neighbor."

THE STATISTICAL CRANK

Of all kinds of cranks the statistical crank is, to ordinary people, the most oppressive. He knows, or pretends to know, the facts and figures about everything. When he was a boy he was said to have had "a head for figures," and was credited with having a "mathematical turn of mind." To him the line of beauty was a row of figures, and the favorite poems of his youth were logarithms. When other boys were engaged in mumble-peg and leap-frog pursuits, he was absorbed with divisors, quotients, and multiplicands in the hilarious pastime of seeing how many vulgar fractions he could get on a slate, and in investigating the cube root of the star route distance between the earth and the planet Mars, or in some other equally unnatural arithmetical dissipation.

The statistical crank can give the figures on anything, from the number of bricks (without straw) that the Israelites made while in Egypt—on the supposition that they worked ten hours a day—to the number of miles that the average woman will walk while looking for her scissors, during an ordinary lifetime.

He is very precise as to details. An ordinary man will tell you that the cotton crop of 1881 was about six million bales. The statistical crank will tell you that it was 5,987,542 bales, averaging 489 lbs. each. His strong point is in telling you how many times something or other, if laid end to end, would reach around the world. One of them told us, the other day, that he had made a calculation which showed that if one issue of *Texas Siftings* was spread out, each copy separately, that a man could walk in a straight line for nineteen and a half miles without getting off the paper. No doubt his calculation was correct, and if we were a carpet factory it might be useful; but as no one except a lunatic would care to walk nineteen and a half miles over a stripe of *Texas Siftings*, in such weather as we are having at present, and as we are not selling our paper by the yard or mile, we cannot see what profit or object there can be in making such calculations.

The statistical crank is very much given to figuring out how much could be done with the money spent in different forms of dissipation, and in the purchase of certain luxuries, provided it was saved and used in some other way. He will tell you how many loaves of bread could be furnished to the poor with the money that could be saved if everybody stopped smoking; or the number of degraded heathen in foreign lands that could each have a Bible laid down, freight prepaid, at their door, with the amount of wealth annually spent in tobacco. He always fails, however, to give you figures regarding the small number of ex-smokers that would be likely to use the money saved from cigars and tobacco, in filling up the poor with loaves, or in adding Bibles to the scanty library of the heathen.

He usually prides himself on having a memory equal to that of Magliabecchi, and when he shuts his eye and elevates his index finger, while he goes down into the recesses of one of his mental pigeon-holes to find the day of the month that Noah landed on Mount Arrarat, and the exact tonnage of the Ark, or some such figures of vital interest, you see him in his most interesting mood and graceful attitude, and if you do not get away right then, on the pretext of having a letter to send off on the northern mail, you will, in all probability, have your mind seriously impaired in

trying to follow his argument that England's suprem-
76 acy is on the wane, "because, sir, her imports exceed
her exports by one million three hundred and seventy
pounds, eleven shillings and eight pence sterling per
annum, sir."

The Hon. F. D. Coburn is one of the most gifted
statistical cranks that we have heard of lately. He
publishes, in the *American Agriculturist*, a calculation in which he shows that if the food annually given
to dogs in the United States was saved, it would feed
286,002 hogs, and these hogs would weigh 85,800,600
pounds of pork, would fill 2,860 freight cars, and
would sell for $4,700,012. He goes on to show that this
money would endow 171 colleges, build 315 hospitals,
or 6,506 schoolhouses, and pay 11,231 school teachers,
and that it would also furnish a hymn-book to every
unconverted sinner in the land.

These calculations have depressed us very much,
for we have always loved dogs, and as we count up
the dogs we owned, and thoughtlessly and wicked-
ly fed, we see visions of unbuilt hospitals, unendowed
colleges, and a depleted free school fund, for all of
which, according to the Hon. Coburn, we are account-
able, and in the future, when we "give our poor dog
a bone," a sense of guilt will steal over us as we realize that we are actually robbing the larder of some
hungry school teacher, and when we give the pup a
plateful of scraps we will feel as if he was gnawing a
collection of short-metre hymns that really belonged
to some hymnless member of an unbuilt church.

DISSATISFIED ENGLISHMEN IN TEXAS

Almost all animals, when transfered to a strange country and climate, will adapt themselves—in habits, mode of life, etc.—to their surroundings. The Englishman is an exception. When he is met in the United States he is at once recognized by a sort of Rule Britannia expression of countenance that he does not attempt to disguise, and by his incessant grumbling. The British Constitution gives every free-born Englishman the right to grumble, and his veneration for the aforesaid British Constitution is only equaled by the tenacity with which he clings to the right accorded him. A great many Britons come to Texas, and suffer dreadful hardships, owing to the fact that Texas differs in many respects from England. There are no fogs, nor paupers, nor incendiary Irishmen in Texas, nor is there a branch office of the London *Times* to write complaints to, so the Englishman on a foreign shore is unhappy.

Thanks to the enterprise of the Sunset Route people
78 and the descriptive eloquence of Dr. Kingsbury, their
agent in England, Western Texas is filling up rapidly
with dissatisfied English immigrants, who come over
here to assist in developing the resources of our State.
After they have been here a few weeks, however,
they are apt to develop a disposition to go back. They
flock to the office of the Sunset Route in San Antonio,
lift up their voices and weep, until Col. Andrews, the
Vice-President of the road, prays fervently that the
day may come when he can lay his hand on Dr. Kingsbury. The lamentations of Jeremiah are joyful carols
compared to the lamentations those Englishmen get
off in Col. Andrews' office.

There is only one place in this world where there is
more wailing, weeping and gnashing of teeth than in
Col. Andrews' office. The other place is in Jerusalem.
There is a portion of the foundation wall of Solomon's
temple still visible in Jerusalem. At certain seasons of
the year, all orthodox Jews from Poland, and other
parts of Europe, make a pilgrimage to that old wall,
and after reciting a mournful litany, they wail, tear
their hair, throw themselves on the ground, and go on
as if they had several large sized red ants concealed
in their underwear. Well, that's the way it is almost
every day in Col. Andrews' office. He gets so mad that
for weeks it is not safe for a San Antonio journalist
to apply to have his pass renewed. The Colonel has a
small bottle full of genuine London fog that he imported, and he allows homesick Englishmen to smell
the bottle. It is said to be a touching sight to see a
florid Englishman, with a mournful look in his tearful
eyes, howling over a pint of the British atmosphere.

Some day we are going to entice Colonel Andrews
out into the woods and persuade him, with a gun, to

tell all he knows about English immigration to Texas, and after we have drawn it all out of him, we shall publish it in book form, and make a fortune out of it.

Our artist has given lifelike portraits of two Englishmen who came to Austin last year. They were arrested while prowling about the suburbs, loaded down with firearms, and asking everybody they met to show them where they could get a shot at a herd of wild buffalo. They were supposed to be insane and dangerous, and our sketch represents the expression of their faces on being disarmed, and told there were no wild buffalo within a thousand miles of Austin.

The dissatisfied English immigrant may be divided into two classes. The contented English immigrant can only be divided into one class. He is not numerous enough to divide into more than one class. There are two distinct kinds of dissatisfied English immigrants. There is, first, the dissatisfied immigrant of high degree, while the other class is composed of those of low degree. The only redeeming feature of the immigrant of low degree is that he is never sober. He is willing, however, be it said to his credit, to do anything for a living except work. It was to get away from anything savoring of toil that he came to Texas. He could get more work than he wanted at home. When he is sick at his stomach, and has no appetite, he goes to Col. Andrews for advice, and when he has got a big appetite he also goes to Col. Andrews for advice, and usually charges the Colonel from a quarter up to five dollars for all such advice. The weather is never at the right temperature, even if he wanted to work.

In the cotton picking season it is too " 'ot," and in the winter it is "too blarsted cold, ye know." What eventually becomes of the dissatisfied English immigrant of low degree is somewhat of a mystery, but there is reason to believe that he goes to swell the

grand army of tramps. He has fine natural qualifications for that business.

The dissatisfied English immigrant of high degree
is an entirely different kind of valuable acquisition.
He makes people believe that he has had a high position in the army, and is closely related to a noble
family of high rank, and he hints that it is a matter
of uncertainty how soon he will fall heir to a princely
fortune and a title. He is correct about this being a
matter of uncertainty. It is very uncertain. The immigrant is charmed with everything he sees in Texas.
He is even charmed with Gibbs, the genial freight
agent, and pats Col. Andrews on the back, and calls
him " 'Arry."

Col. De Berkely, we will call him, for that sounds very
much like his real name, is all the rage for a month
or so, after which he becomes a major-general in the
ranks of dissatisfied English immigrants. He sneers
at New Philadelphia, the Texas Rugby. When in his
cups, he tells Gibbs confidentially that you can see
at a glance that Col. Andrews is not of noble birth—
that there is no style about him. Somebody tells Col.
Andrews what Col. De Berkely has said, and there is
a perceptible coolness. In the meantime, De Berkely
owes large sums to all the San Antonio tradesmen
who were so fortunate as to secure his custom. His
remittances from England are mysteriously delayed
on the road. He imparts family secrets, that involve
royal personages of high degree in England, to San
Antonio saloon keepers, with whom he has credit.
When sober enough to do so, he indites long letters
to leading English papers, denouncing everybody
connected with the Sunset Route, from Col. Pierce to
the humblest brakesman, in consequence of which Dr.
Kingsbury, in London, has to hire a hall and explain
to the aroused British public all about the mosquitoes

at New Philadelphia, and the Texas malaria, which, so Col. De Berkely writes, gets into the legs of the *81* newly-arrived English immigrant. Finally, much to the relief of everybody, except those who advanced him credit and money, Col. De Berkely disappears. It is whispered around that Col. Andrews has had him kidnapped and drowned for saying that he, Andrews, had no style about him; but De Berkely turns up all right in England, where he bewilders poor Kingsbury with a mendacious description of Western Texas.

There are some few Englishmen in Texas who are jolly good fellows, but the most of those who come to Texas are not the kind of immigrants that Texas yearns for.

"PINAFORE" REVIVED

Last week a strapping negro woman was up before an Austin justice, charged with unmercifully beating her boy, a saddle-colored imp.

"I don't understand how you can have the heart to treat your own child so cruelly."

"Jedge, has you been a parent of a wufless yaller boy like dat ar cub of mine?"

"Never—no, never!" ejaculated the judge, with great vehemence, getting red in the face.

"Den don't talk."

There was such a sensation in court that the judge had to call "next" four or five times, and to fine a man who said "Hardly ever," fifty dollars, before order was restored.

The birds that men love, die young.
—Milton

OBITUARY

The day of thanksgiving is past. Our thanksgiving bird is dead. After life's fitful fever he proved to be quite fat. He passed peacefully away on the 23d ultimo, and on the next evening his remains, accompanied by a large circle of appreciative admirers and cranberry sauce, were laid away never more to be seen by mortal eyes. He was a noble specimen of his race, and we who knew him best, loved him for his many excellent qualities. We found him full of generous impulses and stuffing; he had a warm heart, and was liberal to a fault—in the matter of gravy.

The sketch of the deceased, as he lay in the catafalque just prior to the obsequies, was made by our special artist, and we take a sad pleasure in presenting it at the head of this notice. We feel the full force of our bereavement when we realize that we can never look on the original of the picture again. He was born on Onion Creek, in the spring of Anno Domini 1881, spent his early days out in the brush, roosted at night in Judge Tiff Johnson's barnyard, and sometime prior to his death gave almost his undivided attention to a neighbor's sugar cane patch. None knew the deceased more intimately than we did-we were with him in his last moments, and with our own hands performed the last sad rites of tying his legs together. It therefore seems fitting that we should pay this tribute to his worth.

The hapless defunct was cut off in the prime of life, and in the woodshed.

Now, as we stand full of thankfulness, and a large piece of his second joint, we feel that it is our privilege to drop a silent tear in his memory, while our heart is filled with sorrow because there is nothing left of him but...

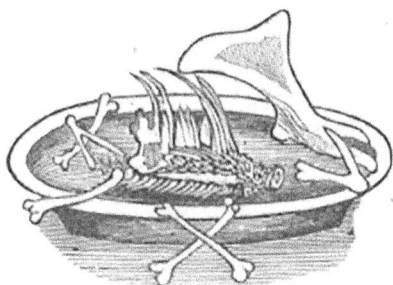

HEAVEN

WHEN poor Artemus Ward, whose heart was as tender as his life was pure, died in England, a touching piece of obituary poetry appeared in a prominent English newspaper, the first lines of which read:

He has gone to the land where there's no laughter,
He who made mirth for us all.

That Browne, for that was his proper name, died in the odor of sanctity we are not prepared to say; but the idea sought to be conveyed in the lines quoted is that he went to the place where the good people usually go, and that it was a land where everything like hilarity was forbidden by city ordinance, as it were. That was the poet's idea of Heaven, and over-looking Browne's humorous career, and his tendency to levity, the poet kindly enrolled him among the citizens of the "land where there's no laughter."

Different people have different ideas of Heaven. Even different bodies of Christians do not agree precisely as to what kind of a place Heaven is. The overworked, worn-out man—and he is in the majority—feels positive that Heaven means rest, and rest means Heaven. The mortal who has suffered from the stings of poverty, can not well separate his idea of Heaven from that of pecuniary independence. To the invalid, Heaven means health. The Indian's idea of Heaven is a happy hunting ground, where there are more buffalo and fewer white men than he finds on this planet. That is what the Indian wants to make him happy. To be perfectly happy, however, he would require an occasional United States soldier to torture

and scalp. Even in Heaven the poor Indian craves for a little amusement. The Moslem's Heaven has been described as being made up principally of black eyes and lemonade? He, too, however, would feel more at home if he were furnished with an occasional "dog of an infidel" to put to the sword, as suggested by the Koran. It is not unlikely that the South Sea Islander's dream of bliss includes a tender young missionary for culinary purposes among the attractions of his Heaven.

Besides having a Heaven fixed up to their own liking, most persons have another place fixed up for the special accommodation of those who do not worship in the same church with them. There is in all men, to a greater or less degree, a latent yearning, to make it unpleasant, both here and hereafter, for those who have the bad taste to dissent from their peculiar views on theological and political topics. Mark Twain illustrated this idea very neatly in his reply to the question as to his belief in eternal punishment. He said that he believed most emphatically in everlasting and eternal punishment, provided he was allowed to pick the men for punishment.

But let us return to "the land where there's no laughter." There are in every denomination of Christians, a great many people who not only believe, but fervently hope that there is a land where there is no laughter, and that they will get to it. There are also many infidels who are cheered up in their earthly pilgrimage by the same hope. There have been saints whose spirits were so lovely and cheerful that they were really too good for this world, and there have been alleged saints who, suffering like Carlyle from indigestion, were more like devils than anything else. Some of the heroes of the Reformation were as vicious as Mahomet himself. These, of course, have no

use for a Heaven where there is anything savoring of
86 good humor. If they ever were to reach Heaven, which
is extremely problematical, and they were to discover
any signs of genuine happiness, they would regard
themselves as having been swindled.

So Artemus Ward has been consigned without his
being consulted, to "the land where there's no laughter." Let us sift this matter a little. Assuming that
there will be a resurrection, and that the good will
inhabit Heaven in the body, let us discard the theories of the followers, and see what the great founder
of Christianity has to say. It will be discovered, according to that high authority, that there will be a
holier sound in Heaven than the chanted litany of the
cowled monk, or the pious war-cries of the Puritan. If
this be not so, then the document on which their chain
of title is based is a sham. Have these wise men who
feel so confident that there is no laughter in Heaven,
forgotten what Christ said about little children? Have
those sacred and comforting words, "and of such is
the Kingdom of Heaven," entirely slipped from their
memories, or do they not know that a little child that
did not laugh would be like a sun that did not shine?
Therefore, most wise and reverend sir, your Master
having put little children, laughter and all, in Heaven,
how are you going to get them out?

*One of the Galveston clergymen recently
preached a thrilling sermon on the wickedness
of Sodom. A stranger from Chicago went out
during the middle of the sermon and shed bitter
tears. The sermon made him homesick. He left on
the next train for Chicago.*

THE TEXAS DESPERADO

The reputation for lawlessness that Texas has among the people of some of the northern and eastern states is not the result of the Sam Bass and Wesley Hardin sort of outlaw and their lawless deeds, but rather the result of the visits that Texas enjoys from the peaceful but imaginative young man who comes from some virtuous eastern city to spend the winter, for the benefit of his health, in Western Texas. Before coming to Texas he has read a good deal of the "One-Eyed Zeke, the Scout," and "Dick, the Desperado," sort of literature. Previous to the packing of his trunk, he provides himself with some guns, a few revolvers, and a double-edged weapon with a spring back and a blade like a hay-knife. The latter he proposes using whenever it may be necessary to cut his way through the jungle, or when fate may put it in his power to rescue some beautiful pale-face maiden from her redskin captors. He has rehearsed the thing so often in his mind, that he knows exactly how the incidents will follow each other in rapid succession—how he will steal up on the unsuspecting sons of the forest as they are preparing to torture their victim; how he will rush in on the foe, and, first cutting the rawhide thongs that bind the captive, turn, and, with his trusty knife, pile up a cord or two of dead Indians; how he will seize the captive maiden—the beautiful Inez de Gonzales, daughter of a Spanish hidalgo—and, vaulting on the back of a coal-black mustang, etc., etc.

He tells the boys at home what be is going to do, and he promises that he will bring back scalps, wampum, wigwams, Indian mounds, and other bric-

88 a-brac, and present them to his friends as mementos of his sojourn in Texas. When he arrives in Texas he is disgusted to find schools, faro-banks, newspapers, church scandals, and other evidences of civilization. To the first man who will buy, he sells some of his revolvers, and secretly drops his hay-knife into a well. He lives a quiet, uneventful life at a boarding-house, where he eats the best canned goods that the market and his landlady can afford for $6 a week, and never meets with any more exciting adventure than being arrested and fined for carrying a pistol.

When his father sends him money enough to buy a railroad ticket, he goes back home in the spring, wearing a broad-brimmed hat—which be ostentatiously calls a sombrero—and jangling a huge pair of Mexican spurs at his heels. This is the time when he develops into the noted Texas desperado—about the only desperado Texas can now lay claim to. Before retiring on the first night of his return home, he asks his mother to just lay a blanket beside a tree-box on the sidewalk, and he will try and borrow an old saddle or a brick for a pillow. He is so accustomed to sleeping in the open air, he says, that be cannot bear the close confinement of a house. When the boys call around for the scalps, Indian mounds and things that he promised to bring them from Texas, he tells them how he lost, in a border foray, a large Saratoga trunk filled with scalps, and a gripsack packed full of wampum and wigwams. Then he gives them a thrilling account of a prairie fire, and how he saved his life by crawling into the carcass of a buffalo he had slain, until the fire passed over and exhausted itself. After this he recounts a desperate encounter he had with a stagerobber, and gives a detailed and hair-curdling description of a scene at a lynching, where he got the drop on the crowd, and rescued the doomed **89** man. His conversation bristles with profanity, and is saturated with gore. The writer of this has been ten years in Texas, has been among the chivalrous Mexicans on the Rio Grande, the aesthetic cowboys on the plains, and the wild and hilarious church members in the cities, and has not yet seen a single pistol fired with intent to injure a human being, nor has he ever seen a buffalo goring Sunday-school children on the streets on any city of Texas; and the only genuine, blood-thirsty desperado he has seen was the young man above described.

Of course there are some lawless and desperate men in Texas, but none of them equals the tenderfoot from the east for cold-blooded ferocity—after he gets back home.

Talmage says "men of talent and commanding intellect are never good dancers." That is the first time we have seen any public allusion to our awkwardness in dancing.

MEXICAN BULLFIGHTS

This is the season of the year when the Mexicans on the Rio Grande improve their minds with *fiestas*. The redeeming features of the *fiesta* are drunkenness, gambling and bull-fighting. But occasionally they fight with knives, besides. Another redeeming feature is that while the *fiesta* is going on, the Mexicans have not got any time to waste in expediting the ranches of their stock. Expedite is a Star-Route term, and means to steal. Nobody can gamble, get drunk, go to bullfights, and steal ponies at one and the same time, and the Mexican who tries it is likely to neglect some of his duties. At Laredo and El Paso, owing to the completion of railroads to those points, the Mexicans have received considerable assistance from the Americans in properly celebrating the *fiestas*. There were, perhaps, not so many Americans, but they helped a great deal. They are very willing. It takes five or six Mexicans to get as drunk and make as much fuss as one hardy Anglo-Saxon. The latter throws more soul into the performance. He can be heard several miles off.

The most peculiar feature of the *fiesta* is the bullfight, which takes place in an amphitheater built for
the purpose. It will hold a great many people, probably as many as can get into it. The board fence that
separates the audience from the arena is so arranged
that the bullfighter can climb up on it where the bull
cannot reach him. This fence enables the bullfighter
to show his contempt for danger,and he makes liberal
use of his opportunities. The bullfighters are dressed
in all the colors of the rainbow. They look very much
like the face cards of the pack enlarged. It is really
funny to see the jack of diamonds, the king of hearts,
and all the rest of the royal family that are so familiar to many of our readers, prancing about the arena

In reality, there is no bullfight at all. There is more
real danger in lighting a kerosene lamp, or in calling
a policeman a liar, than there is in a dozen bullfights.
Before the bull is presented with the freedom of the
arena, several inches of his horns are sawed off. As
with some folks we know of, it hurts the bull to have
his horns cut off. If a heroic bullfighter should lose his
presence of mind, and in his efforts to get out of the
arena run against the bull, a dull horn is the kind of a
horn the reckless daredevil wants to run against; but
there is no danger of that. The horns are sawed off
down to the quick, and are actually bloody.

The end of the horn is as sensitive to the bull as an
army-sized boil is to a man. If a man has a large boil
on his person, he does not try to butt people with it.
On the contrary, he is very careful that nobody hits
against it. That's the way it is with the bull with the
sore horn. Instead of rushing about, trying to impale
the bullfighter, the bull is half scared to death for
fear the jack of spades or the king of hearts may
accidentally bump against that sore horn. This is the

kind of a bull the Mexicans love to fight. The jack
92 of diamonds, knowing this, gets right in front of the
dangerous brute, which turns tail, for fear the face
card will run against that sore horn. Perhaps some
of our readers know that it hurts to run against the
jack of diamonds, particularly if hearts are trumps,
and the other fellow has the right bower, and perhaps the ace and the ten-spot; but we are digressing.

As soon as the bull refuses to hurt his sore horn
against the jack of hearts, the air is rent with vi-
vas in honor of the reckless intrepidity of the bull
fighter, who gracefully bows his acknowledgments.
All the bullfighters try in vain to bump against that
sore horn but the bull is too smart for them. They
punch him with spears, thrust sharp spikes festooned
with tissue paper in his hide, until he is dripping with
blood; until the unfortunate brute is exhausted; but he
never loses his presence of mind so much as to punch
one of the face cards with that sore horn. The animal
is finally roped, the spikes are pulled out of his hide,
and he is either driven out of the arena, or butchered.

The Mexican bullfight is a beautiful blending of
Spanish cruelty and Indian cowardice. No decent
American would sit through the whole performance.
If he really needed an emetic, he would go to a drug
store and get one.

COYOTES

The coyote is about two-thirds the size of a yellow dog, and looks like a second-hand wolf in straightened circumstances. He bears about the same relation to the genuine wolf that the buzzard does to the eagle, or that a chicken thief does to a modern bank cashier. He has a perpetual air of being ashamed of himself, or of something he has done. As you catch a glimpse of him, trotting away from one matt of timber to another, looking back over his ears, and with his tail furled around his left leg, he looks as if he were aware that the police had a clue to his whereabouts, and were working up his case. No one ever saw a fat coyote.

94 You may catch a young one, civilize him as much as you can, feed him on canned groceries, and put a brass collar on him, but his ribs will still be his most prominent feature, and at the first favorable opportunity he will voluntarily and ungratefully leave your hospitable roof, and from choice, become a roving vagabond on the prairie, living on carrion and sharing his meal with the buzzard. These predatory shadows are not at all dangerous. There is no fight in them. They are fatal to sheep when the coyote majority is forty to a minority of one sick sheep, but otherwise they are quite harmless.

What they lack in courage they make up in craftiness. They will twist themselves into all manner of grotesque postures, and tumble around in the long grass, that the rabbit or young fawns may, by curiosity, be induced to come within reach of their sharp fangs. This last playful characteristic of the coyote was described to us by a friend, who was a New York newspaper reporter, and acquainted with a coyote that resided in a cage in Central Park. His statement may, therefore, be relied on, even to the length of the grass.

The coyote has a small head and fox-like ears, but the biggest end of him is his voice. The mellifluous, silver-toned euphony of one of his nocturnal overtures would scare a monkey off a hand organ, and make an Italian opera singer hang himself with envy, and one of his own chords. When he slinks up, and, seating himself in the twilight of a camp-fire on the prairie, opens out with a canticle and runs up the scale—starting with a diminuendo whine, throwing in a staccato shriek, and ending with a crescendo howl—the sonorific outburst terrifies the Genus of Acoustics, and makes the welkin ring until it cracks itself and has to be carried off and repaired.

A hardy frontiersman, traveling over the boundless prairies of western Texas, when the shades of night **95** are beginning to fall, prepares to camp for the night. He stakes out his tired steed to graze on the flower-bespangled grass, while he prepares his frugal meal. Having placed his weapons within easy reach, he spreads his blankets, and stretching his weary limbs, resigns himself to the care of the drowsy god. Suddenly the air is alive with direful yells, shrieks and howls, as if all the Indians on the American continent had been turned loose. Does the hardy frontiersman spring to his feet, seize his trusty rifle, and prepare to sell his life as dearly as possible? He does not. He merely turns over and mutters drowsily, "d—n a coyote, anyhow," for he knows that of all the wild beasts that roam the jungle, the coyote is the most harmless.

One coyote at night can make enough noise to induce the inexperienced traveler to believe that there are at least fifty of them in the immediate neighborhood. If a coyote was assayed, we venture to predict that he would be found to consist of one part wolf and nine parts of vocal ability. The only time when the voice of the coyote, as one of the resources of Texas, has any value, is when it is used to take the conceit out of some smart stranger from the Eastern States. The acclimated Texan induces the stranger to go with him in pursuit of game, and to camp out on the prairie or in the woods, and he enjoys the stranger's fear when he hears the coyotes for the first time as they howl around the camp-fire in "the dead waste and middle of the night." It is difficult to convince the stranger that the coyote will not make a meal of him and eat his horse and baggage for dessert. In fact, it is not the policy of the Texan to convince the stranger.

That this popular fallacy regarding the ferocity of the coyote exists, was illustrated not long since in the remarks made by a Northern preacher, in a sermon he preached shortly after his arrival in the State. He was illustrating how the heedless sinner refused to benefit by the most earnest warning, in the very presence of the wrath to come. He said: "Dear friends, methinks I see two men walking out on one of your bee-utiful prairies. They enjoy the perfume of the flowers, the songs of the innocent little birds, and the calm, quiet beauty of your glorious Indian summer evenings. Communing together, they walk along heedless of danger. The sun sinks to rest beyond the distant horizon; the curtain of night gradually descends and closes out the light of day; still the two men walk leisurely along, feeling safe and secure. But, hark! What sound is that in the distance? What blood-curdling howl makes them arrest their steps? It is, dear friends—it is the cry of the wolves on their track—the fierce and bloodthirsty coyote in hot pursuit, ah! And what think you do these two unfortunate men do? One of them, my beloved congregation, realized his danger, and running to a tree, climbed up by the aid of a convenient branch, out of reach of the cruel fangs of the relentless beasts of prey. He called unto his companion and said unto him: 'O, my brother, reach out and take hold of this branch, climb up here beside me, and be saved!' But the other said: 'No, there is no danger; the wolves are still a long way off—I have time enough.' Alas! dear hearers, while he was yet speaking, the dreadful coyotes came upon him, and, rending him limb from limb, devoured him even in the twinkling of an eye. Thus it is, O, careless and heedless sinners, that you, tonight, stand, etc., etc."

When the preacher concluded the services and was

leaving the church, he was accosted by old man Parker, (who has lived in Texas since '36), who said: **97** "Parson, the front end of your discourse was grand and gloomy, and calculated to bluff the unconverted sinner. You had a full hand, and might have raked in all the mourners in the pot; but, Lord bless your soul, you played a nine spot when you chipped in with that wolf yarn. Yes, Doctor, you played hell when you got on that coyote lay!"

A NEWS FACTORY

We have often wondered how it was that the St. Louis *Globe-Democrat* exhibited so much more enterprise than our most enterprising Texas papers, in publishing special telegrams descriptive of murders and other crimes committed in Texas. We have frequently read of Texas murders and robberies in the *Globe-Democrat*, that we never saw mentioned in any Texas paper. Now we understand how it was done. The feline has been ejected from the bag, and we can explain what has so long been a mystery.

In the *Globe-Democrat* office there is kept a number of stereotyped forms, like the following, with blank spaces in them:

ANOTHER MURDER IN TEXAS.
[SPECIAL DESPATCH TO THE *GLOBE-DEMOCRAT*.]

_____, TEXAS. — A cold-blooded murder was committed here ____ day, about ____ o'clock in the __. Mr. _____ _____, a peaceable citizen, was called to his door, seized and carried a short distance from the house, and shot dead. No clue to the murderers. The country is in a very disturbed state, and life and **98** property unsafe.

THE KNIFE IN TEXAS.
[SPECIAL DESPATCH TO THE *GLOBE-DEMOCRAT*.]

_____, TEXAS. — Two men named _____ and _____, met last , in the ____ saloon at this place. After drinking together they got into a quarrel, and ____ stabbed _____ in the body ___ times. _____ is not expected to recover.

DAILY RECORD OF TEXAS STAGE ROBBERIES.
[SPECIAL DESPATCH TO THE *GLOBE-DEMOCRAT*.]

_____, TEXAS. — The stage between _____ and _____, was stopped and robbed _____day by ___ masked men. The passengers, __ in number, contributed $____ and __ watches. The mails were _____. The robbers are supposed to be the same who robbed the _____ stage the day before.

Every night the managing editor calls the foreman up, and a conversation something in this style takes place:

"Got nearly all the copy you want?"

"All but about a column, sir."

"Got all your suicides and fearful accidents in?"

"Yes, sir."

"Have you enough clerical scandals and dreadful outrages for this issue?"

"I believe we have fully the usual number."

"Well, then, l reckon you had better fill up with Texas crimes. Gimme them stereotypes. Here, fill up the blanks in this 'Dreadful Murder;' any names will do. Locate it at Dallas; we have not had a murder there for a week. And here's the 'Stage Robbery' blank; locate the scene somewhere near San Antonio. It might as well go in every day, and twice in the Sunday edition. And you can use this 'Lynching' form; it'll fit any

Texas town. By the way, you had better get a new stereotype of that; the old one has been used so often **99** it's pretty badly worn. Now, I think that will about fill your column, but if it don't, why, just stick in a homicide, a commutation by Gov. Roberts, or any other crime that we have got blanks for."

"Yes, sir."

"Texas is a great State, and she deserves all the prominence we can give her."

PATRONIZING SUBSCRIBER

The patronizing subscriber is the most exasperating man with whom the journalist has to deal. He does not hand two dollars to the editor, and request that the paper be sent to his address for a year. He is not that sort of a man.

When he buys a railroad ticket he pays cash down to the clerk who edits the ticket with a hand stamp; and to the Chinese journalist who edits his shirt with a flat-iron he disburses some of his wealth before he gets his shirt. But when he patronizes the editor, his tactics are different. He says: "Well, I reckon you'd better put my name down for your paper. I really take more papers now than I read, but I suppose I'll have to take yours, too. We are all expected to do something toward supporting the press, you know." He says this with the air of a philanthropist subscribing for the controlling interest in a narrow-gage railroad, or a new church, on which he never expects to draw a dividend; but, at the same time, he neglects to reduce his cash balance by subscribing the $2 in advance. He tells the editor to call on him for the amount when

he needs it. He is careful to leave the impression that
100 he has no possible use for the paper, and he will likely
never read it, but he merely wants to help the editor
out with the two dollars he does not pay.

Although the patronizing subscriber does not
contribute a cent, he positively imagines he has
squandered money that should have gone to the really deserving poor. In time, as the paper prospers,
he comes to regard himself as the founder and chief
proprietor of it. The only wonder is that he does not
sell it out when, as is frequently the case, it fails to
reflect his political and religious views. When an editorial demolishes one of his pet theories, he begins
to regret that he has been nourishing a serpent in
his bosom, and talks of withdrawing his support from
the paper. He even hints at establishing an independent organ that will properly represent the people. In
return for the copy, that he has not yet paid for, the
exacting patron expects that the editor will attempt,
in some slight degree, to pay off the national debt of
obligation due to him, by bringing his name before
the people as a suitable man for some prominent position. If this is not done he regards it as an evidence
of base ingratitude.

He comes into the editorial room with a manuscript
describing the wonderful idiosyncrasies of character
displayed by his house dog, or some other such matter
of national importance, and wants it put in the paper;
and when the editor reads it, and suggests that his
columns are crowded and that he hardly thinks the
matter offered would interest the subscribers anyhow, the patronizing subscriber is astonished, and
says: "My Heavens, man, ain't I a subscriber?" and
then he goes off determined to bestow his patronage
on some live paper that will appreciate his assistance.

What exasperates him most, is for the editor to send him a bill for the $2 of capital stock that stands op- *101* posite his name on the books. We regret that these few words will not reach the patronizing subscriber, because that kind of philanthropist does not read *Texas Siftings*, except when he borrows or steals a copy. Our invariably-in-advance policy is very distasteful to him.

THE HORNED FROG

He stood on the Pacific slope of Onion Creek, near a small schoolhouse. He was evidently the school master. His rusty black clothes and spacious shirt collar betrayed him. He was gazing intently on a small object on the ground. As we approached he picked it up, and holding it out in his hand, asked us if we had ever seen an *iguanian* reptile of the *genus phynosomna*. We confessed that we had never seen one often enough to get intimately acquainted with its domestic habits.

He said that it was a very interesting reptile, and was vulgarly called the horned frog. The specimen in his hand was the first we had ever seen, and the teacher discoursed learnedly regarding the manners and customs and family history of the bright-looking little reptile.

We have since seen many of the frogs, and have found them to be very much of an improvement on the bullfrog, although their vocal ability is much more limited. When the horned frog is at home he indulges in wild bursts of eloquent silence, and seldom makes

any noise, except when you lock him up in a bureau
102 drawer to see how long he will live without food.

The horned frog is a native of Texas and Lower California, where he is found inhabiting the sandy soil of the prairies, and the pockets of the small boy.

The horned frog is really not a frog at all, but a lizard traveling incognito. He is shorter and broader than the ordinary lizard, grey in color, with bright spots and horny spikes all over his back, and on his head two real horns about half-an-inch in length. He is not as big as a bull, but you can take him by the horns all the same.

Although the horned frog does not live in a restaurant, he eats about as many flies as if he did; in fact, he lives on flies; that is his principal pursuit. When he eats a fly he knows what he is doing, and that is where he has a great advantage over the regular restaurant boarder. We have seen horned frogs used as fly traps in grocers' windows. The fly that succeeds in attracting the attention of a horned frog can never be used afterwards.

The horned frog is a dry, cleanly little reptile, and seems to have no vices. As he never gets drunk, nor eats hot biscuits, nor runs a newspaper, he is hard to kill. He will live six months without food and be good-natured all the time.

He travels a great deal, but never brags about it. We knew one that left Texas, and three weeks afterwards was registered in a town in the south of England, in the enjoyment of fine health. He traveled cheaply, too; and—although he did not go on an editorial excursion, yet his traveling expenses, including hotel bills, fees to waiters, and other incidentals, only amounted to ten cents, this being the value of the postage stamps pasted on the paper collar box he was mailed in. Large quantities of him were formerly exiled to the Northern States and elsewhere, *103* through the medium of the post-office department. The post-office authorities did not object much to the horned frog, but after a while they found that tarantulas, centipedes and an occasional rattlesnake were to be found among the letters and other mail matter. The paper boxes in which these little playthings were forwarded frequently got broken, and the foundling tarantula would occasionally bear away a post-office clerk to the dark and silent tomb. The consequence was that the clerks took to distributing and assorting mails with long poles. This occupied too much time, and when they found any specimens of native Texans, instead of picking them up, placing them in the boxes and re-addressing them, they killed them in their tracks.

About this time life insurance companies began to put extra clauses in their policies, requiring the policyholders to abstain from working in powder mills, from stealing ponies and from handling the mails from Texas. All of which caused the post-office department to pass a constitutional amendment requiring the sender of such insects to kill them before mailing them, as the labor of attending to the matter took up too much of the time of the employees. The horned frog—in which there is no more malice than there is in a cauliflower—had to suffer for the sins of the tarantula, the centipede, the rattlesnake and other representative characters.

2 out of every 3 schoolboys in Texas carry a few horned frogs alive in their pockets during the spring season—for what reason or purpose I am unable to state. But who can give a reason for half the things that a small boy treasures about his person?

THAT TYPICAL TEXAN

Some man whose head was flat—probably ourselves—has said that the North had been hating an ideal Southerner, who never existed; that the South had been hating an ideal Yankee, who never existed; and the Americans generally had been worshiping an ideal Indian, who never existed, except in Fenimore Cooper's novels. We may add to the list of mythical personages an ideal Texan, who figures so largely in the Northern mind and dime novels, but otherwise is as hard to find as Charlie Ross. The typical Texan is a large-sized Jabberwock, a hairy kind of gorilla, who is supposed to reside on a horse. He is half alligator, half human, who eats raw buffalo, and sleeps out on a prairie. He is expected to carry four or five revolvers at his belt, as if he were a sort of perambulating gun rack. He also carries a large assortment of cutlery in his boot. It is believed that a failure to invite him to drink is more dangerous than to kick a can of dynamite. The only time the typical Texan is supposed to be peaceable is after he has killed all his friends, and can find no fresh material to practice on.

It is also the belief in the North that all the Texans are typical Texans, it being utterly impossible for a Texan to be anything except a desperado. Now, we propose to knock this typical Texan, who is accused of being particularly numerous in Western Texas, right off his pins. We are prepared to prove a complete *alibi* for him. We will show that the typical Texan is as mild as picnic lemonade. It will be remembered that stage robbing had been carried on for some time in Western Texas. There are only nine stage robbers in jail at San *105* Antonio now, and the Lord knows how many on the outside. Why, at one time, the traveling public became so accustomed to going through the usual ceremonies that they complained to the stage company if they came through unmolested. Being robbed, came to be regarded as a vested right. On one occasion the stage driver happened to stop his horses right in front of the old Alamo, that sacred Thermopylae that is now being used to store cabbages and potatoes in, right in the heart of San Antonio, where most of the saloons are, in order to give a man on horseback a light for his pipe. As soon as the stage halted, the passengers tumbled out, pell-mell, and, falling in line, held up their hands, and called out, "Don't shoot!"

The point is this: Notwithstanding the stage was robbed so often when there were typical Texans in it, in no instance did any of them violate the law by discharging pistols, or even by using strong language. They never even said: "Why, damme, 'tis too bad!" until the robbers—probably missionaries from the North—had gone away. Does this look like rowdyism? The typical Texan acted more in accordance with the teachings of the New Testament, where it requires the plundered party, who has been robbed of his coat, to pull off his pants, and tender them also to the needy highwayman. It will be seen at once that great injustice has been done our people. There is, however, a world of consolation in the fact that in Missouri, where three crops of guerrillas and bushwhackers are raised every year, a bogus Jesse James and a few assistants rob a whole train.

There is also much solid comfort to Texans in the fact that in Arkansaw, where the Arkansaw tooth-

106 pick grows to be as big as a scythe, that lately four beardless boys collected four thousand dollars' worth of money, jewelry and pistols from a train full of passengers. But what has become of the typical Texan? Governor Roberts should offer a reward for a live specimen. Even the stage robbers are not as dangerous as a kerosene lamp to handle. When an officer of the law comes across a Texas stage robber, and says: "Oh, wake up, William Riley, and come along with me!" William invariably drops his little pop-gun and other playthings, and goes along with him.

HE WANTED A NOTICE

"Are you the editor?" said a man, who wore a conciliatory smile and a dyed beard, as he took a seat in our office.

We acknowledged that at present we served and instructed the public in that capacity, and "to prove our assertion, we showed him the blisters made on our hands by our exertions in operating the Archimedean lever that moves the world.

"Well, I want you to surprise me with a flattering personal notice in your paper. I'm going to run for constable in the eighth ward, and I want something neat in the way of a send-off."

"Our columns are always open to advance the best interests of the public, but we shall expect you to first surprise us with a pecuniary compensation, not necessarily for publication, but merely as a pledge of good faith."

"I'll pay. A man can't expect to be surprised without paying for it in advance. What have you got?"

"We can accommodate you with almost any kind of personal notice, from a cheap electro-plated biography to an 18-caret obituary, and at a scale of prices varying according to the amount of strain on our columns and veracity. In moulding public opinion we defy competition. Now, how would you like this? It is a neat little pre-Raphaelite gem, and will cost you only $2.00:

> Our enterprising townsman, Col. B., than whom there is no more popular and genial gentleman in the length and breadth of our great empire state, has consented, at the earnest solicitation of many friends, to sacrifice his very profitable private business for the public good, and has authorized us to announce him as a candidate far the honorable office of constable of this precinct.

"If that is not strong enough, here is a Michael Angelo, full length, in which your good qualities of head and heart will be touchingly alluded to, and you will be commended for your generous impulses—only $5 each insertion. Then we have a brilliant thing, after Mozart, which is really intended for gubernatorial candidates—speaks of your simplicity of character, jean clothes and pay-as-you-go proclivities—but it can easily be modified to suit a prospective constable. It will cost you $7.50. There are several others from $5.00 to $10.00 each. For referring to you as an old landmark, one dollar extra is charged."

"I reckon you can saw me off five dollars' worth, but you must throw in something about my brilliant war record."

"We always do that."

108   "And just wind up by surprising Captain Bill Smike. He is running against me. I wouldn't say anything he might take offense at. Only say he is not fit for the office, because he has a breath like a buzzard, and the record of a convict. You might add that *my* brother hasn't got a wife that has fits. That will hit him where he is sore, for his brother's wife is subject to fits. I don't care to lug any personalities into this campaign unless I am obliged to."

"We can't do it, colonel. Your rival is our personal friend. He is a subscriber."

"Pshaw! I thought you were running an independent paper in the interest of the people, but I see you are the subsidized organ of a political clique," and off he went to see the editor of the other paper.

"You smoke a great deal, Gus," said a friend to Gus DeSmith.

"Yes," replied Gus; "particularly after dinner. I have got so in the habit of smoking after dinner that the dinner don't taste right when I eat it, unless I have a smoke afterwards."

THE EDITORIAL CRANK

The Editorial Crank shows his crankiness in many ways. He suffers most from sensitiveness and solemnity. His mind moves along in a groove, and should it, by accident, be forced out of the groove, it wanders aimlessly around until he sometimes loses it.

Of politics he only knows the good things that the party he belongs to has done or is going to do, and the wicked things that the other party has done or is about to do. His forte is in controversies with other Editorial Cranks. Another editor has probably remarked that bungstarters were first invented in the year 709, B. C., and used by the ancient Egyptians as instruments of warfare. Crank No. 1, in a labored editorial, three and a half feet long, demonstrates that Crank No. 2 has displayed lamentable lack of knowledge of ancient history, and suggests that he should go to a night-school and grind the wire edge off his ignorance; and he concludes by proving (quoting authorities) that it was not as instruments of warfare that bungstarters were used by the ancient Egyptians, B. C., 709; that there were no ancient Egyptians 110 B. C., 709, and that the bungstarter was not invented until the fall of A. D., 211, when Geta, brother to Caracalla, reigned at Rome, and was murdered by his brother, who used for that purpose the first bungstarter ever invented. He surmises that his ignorant brother has confounded the Egyptian word meaning war-chariot, which is similar in sound, with the modern English word, bungstarter.

Then Crank No. 2 answers back and proves the correctness of his assertion by quoting authorities, and by speaking disrespectfully of the intelligence of his learned contemporary, Crank No. 1.

And so the controversy goes on, two columns a week for half-a-year, until the readers get tired, and one day the sheriff has more to do with the paper than the editor has. Here is a sample of the sort of "argument" the crank uses when he has his sleeves rolled up and is earnestly striving to mould public opinion and educate the masses.

The editor of the Emory *Argus*, in the last issue of his paper, throws a ray of sunshine in the path of a contemporary. He says: "From our lofty eminence we look down and smile contemptuously upon the little donkey who edits the Wills Point *Local*, floundering in the dirt and doing his best to throw mud on us."

Egotism is what afflicts the Editorial Crank most. He fails to recognize the fact, that the general public does not care anything about the origin of bungstarters, nor about the other things he writes of to show his learning, nor are they interested in his disputes with other editors about nothing. He is very sensitive. He cannot stand or understand a joke. When a brother editor indulges in some good natured jest at his expense, he gets angry and says spiteful things in reply.

THE CONFIDENTIAL BORE

Of all the great family of bores the confidential bore is the worst. All the rest are mere little post holes, as it were, while he is a 1,200 foot artesian well of a bore. The confidential bore is of all ages and sizes, and flourishes in every climate. He can easily be recognized by the following peculiarities. He always has what he considers a good thing to tell you, but he wants to impart it privately, and, therefore, beckons you to step aside. Then he begins by stating that he does "not want it to go any farther," and, while he is telling you a scrap of scandal about one of his neighbors, or giving you a detailed account of the symptoms attending the teething of his "next to the youngest," of no earthly interest to any but himself and the suffering child, he pokes his fingers in your ribs and stutters with his left eye, when he comes to what he thinks the thrilling, humorous, or impressive part of the narrative.

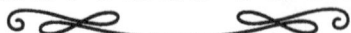

The confidential bore always pokes his victim in the
112 ribs at the crescendo part of his exhaustive drivel, and
when he approaches the fortissimo part he pushes
him clear off the sidewalk. A miserable victim of one
of these confidential outrages is known to have been
driven once around a block and into a saloon, while
being inflicted with the description of the successful
castings and manufacture of a sweet potato pie constructed by some female member of the bore's family.
One of the marked characteristics of the confidential
bore is his weak memory. He will give you a second,
and often a third dose of the same old, uninteresting,
personal reminiscences, forgetting that he has ever
mentioned the matter before. Then, after giving you
some points on a matter that he says will surprise
the people when it becomes public, but that is, for
the present, to be considered "between ourselves, *sub
rosa*, you know," he will go down and lie in wait at the
post-office for some other unfortunate acquaintance,
and tell the same thing to him.

The confidential bore may be a farmer, or a policeman, or a legislator, or a stage robber, but he is never
a successful business man. In the nature of things he
could not be, for he has no idea of the value of time.
There are other members of the great bore family—
the taciturn, the loquacious, the political, and the
clerical bore for instance—that we shall discuss hereafter.

LAVANBURG'S SUBSTITUTE

One afternoon not long since, three or four gentlemen were comfortably seated in the *Texas Siftings* office, very busily engaged in swapping improbable lies about the late war, and explaining to their own satisfaction, why it was that the Confederacy was not such a permanent success as had been anticipated. The discussion drifted into the fighting qualities of the different nationalities. One of the party said that while both sides displayed great gallantry, there was one man in the Confederate army who was spoiling for a fight more than all the rest of the combatants put together. He wanted to get at the Yankees and tear them to pieces, and it was utterly impossible to fill him up with gore.

"What was the name of the patriot?"

114 "I never knew his real name. He was a foreigner who joined our regiment at Brownsville. He was a deserter from Maximillian's army, and we used to call him Lavanburg's substitute."

"What did you call him that for?"

"Because that was precisely what he was. He was Lavanburg's substitute. Brownsville was at that time the only live city in the Confederacy. Thousands of bales of cotton arrived daily, and immense fortunes were made. The town was loaded right up to the muzzle like a public spirited 4th of July cannon, not with gun cotton, but with sons of guns of cotton speculators. Col. Duff, the Confederate post commander, put guards around the town one morning early, and compelled every adult male inhabitant to come up to the captain's office, and exhibit his credentials why he was not busy in the tented field picking out a conspicuous place for his bones to bleach. There was more weeping and wailing and cursing among the Brownsville Israelites than at any time since the siege of Jerusalem. Among these who were led captive up to headquarters at Fort Brown was Lavanburg. He was negotiating for a lot of cotton, which he was afraid another Israelite would gobble up if he let the owner out of sight, so when he, Lavanburg, was told by his escort, myself, that he would probably start on foot for Virginia to assist in the capture of Washington City, he was very much impressed. But he did not kneel down and pray for the success of the Confederacy. I had my eye on him, and if he had done so, I should have noticed it."

"Well, what about his substitute?"

"The only thing left for Lavanburg to do was to procure a substitute to furnish the bones to bleach on some historic battlefield. Lavanburg was perfectly willing to hire a substitute, and allow him to furnish *115* the bones, but there was none in the market. Bones had 'riz' in consequence of the demand. As luck would have it, just at this crisis, a French deserter from Maximillian's army came across the river at Brownsville. He had a full set of bones, and he agreed to strew them himself, if Lavanburg would shell out $400 in gold. So Lavanburg's substitute was conscripted into my company—very good company it was, too."

"Well, tell us about Lavanburg's substitute."

"He was a little bit of a weazened up, black eyed, blackbearded Frenchman, but the way he could go through the bayonet exercise was worth paying admission to behold. To see him form himself into a hollow square and resist a cavalry charge, then turn a back handed somersault through the air, alight on his feet, and hurl back an imaginary hostile brigade, was so terribly realistic—so very like the ghastly reality of war, that some of the officers seriously thought of sending in their resignations; for up to that time, the only hot fire we had been under very much was the campfire. We were 1,500 miles from the hireling foe, and couldn't get any farther away without going into Mexico."

"Well, but what about Lavanburg's substitute?"

"He got to be very popular with the officers. He used to salute them by presenting arms when they rode past. The Texas soldiers did not go much on style. If an officer of high rank rode past a Texas boy on guard, and he happened to see the officer of rank, he would stop playing cards, or whatever else he was doing, and call out: 'I say, Colonel, come over here and give me a chaw of tobacco.' And if the Colonel said he didn't have any, the stern sentinel on the watch tower

of duty would reply 'Well, why in the hell haven't you
116 got some?'

"But that was not the way Lavanburg's substitute
stood guard. He always walked his post and kept so
wide awake that the Yankees would have a hard time
getting into camp unobserved. When an officer appeared, he brought his gun to a present. The officers
liked that, and would ride past him a dozen times a
day, and occasionally the Colonel would stop and talk
to him, like Napoleon conversing familiarly with
one of his old guard. I heard George Caldwell, who
was adjutant, and now lives in San Antonio, tell Tom
Brackenridge, who was major, that if there were a
couple of hundred Lavanburg substitutes in the regiment, instead of being on the Rio Grande, we would be
in Washington City, or New York, guarding Federal
prisoners. Major Brackenridge replied that the failure of Confederate soldiers to present arms to their
superior officers was the real cause of European na-
tions failing to recognize the Confederacy."

"That's very interesting, but why don't you tell us
something about Lavanburg's substitute? Did he find
a convenient place where he could bleach his bones?"

"I'll get there before the break up. One day he and
another soldier got to fooling with sabers. Lavan
burg's substitute got excited. His eyes stuck out, his
hair stood up on end, and he looked for all the world
like a black, hairy tarantula that had been stirred up,
and the consequence was that the Texas soldier got
stuck in the arm. The rest of the soldiers were very
indignant, but the officers said that there would be no
discipline left if Lavanburg's substitute was not encouraged, and they threatened the wounded man with
the guard-house. Shortly after that, while in winter
quarters, Lavanburg's substitute, in describing the

assault on the Malakoff, seized a gun, jumped upon the second tier of bunks, shouting: 'Vive la France!' *117* bayonetted a pair of new saddle-bags worth $1,700 in Confederate money, new issue, and cocking his gun, fired, and shot a piece out of Corporal Burney's ear, who was trying to escape. Heretofore it was only the officers who admired him, but after that the whole regiment respected him so much that they talked about taking him out and hanging him. In fact, some of the soldiers asked what was the use of keeping the regiment where the Yankees couldn't find it, if they were to be slaughtered in detail by a cranky substitute. Some of the boys went home on a furlough and haven't got back yet."

"Did the substitute ever get a chance at the Federal army?"

"Yes, at Indianola. There were three thousand Federals there under Gen. Warren. The substitute was very much distressed because there were not more. He wanted to make up for the lost time during which he had not slaughtered any hostile foe. He was sent out on picket duty. The first chance he had he made a break for the town, and that was the last we ever saw of Lavanburg's substitute."

"He was probably killed by the Federals."

"Well, I'm not sure about it. A prisoner we captured afterwards told us that a deserter from our side, who answered the substitute's description very well, had drawn his bounty as a Federal recruit, and was acting orderly for Gen. Warren."

A TEXAS MUSTANG

When the foreigner pictures a Texas mustang in his mind's eye, he thinks of a noble jet black horse, small and compactly built, with an arched neck, a flowing mane, and a prodigal wealth of a tail. He gets his idea from reading the Mayne Reid class of illustrated lies of border life, where the "noble courser of the prairies" is represented as performing extraordinary feats in carrying his rider beyond the reach of a band of pursuing savages, who are left behind on the frontier of the picture. In the illustrations the mustang has a flashing eye, a distended nostril, a 1:39½ gait, and a tail that reaches to the southwestern corner of the chromo. These pictures, and the ghastly realities that exist on the Texas prairies, remind one of the gigantic pomological specimens, rich in color and juicy looking, that are painted on the outside of a can of preserved strawberries, and of the poor little pale, dwarfed berries inside.

The mustang is a species of horse, angular as a rail fence, and without a pedigree. A difference of opinion exists as to his origin. Some say that he is of Spanish origin—descended from the horses brought from Spain by Cortez during the conquest of Mexico, while others are strongly of opinion that the original father of the race was a clothes-horse, and the female *fons et origo* a nightmare. From the fact that the mustang is destitute of blood, and taking into account his architectural construction, we are inclined to believe that the latter conjecture is the correct one.

He averages about fourteen hands in height. He has large ears, a long head, short mane, and burs in *119* his tail, He is seldom fat, has a protracted body, thin shoulders and hams, and looks not unlike a section of a railroad trestle. In a late paper we read a description of a Texas mustang, by Rev. W. H. Murray, the celebrated Boston preacher. Brother Murray's mustang is the kind that thrives only in the "Frontier Scout" class of literature. When the preacher wrote the description referred to, he took such a grip on truth, and stretched it so far, that away off here in Austin we heard it crack.

The genuine Texas mustang is a parody on the horse, but he is a very useful animal, nevertheless. In driving cattle he is more active and valuable than a large horse would be; and in the matter of shaking up the liver of an invalid, who has been ordered to take horseback exercise for his health, the Texas mustang is a triumphant success.

THE TUMBLE-BUG

The foreigner in Texas is frequently astonished as he drives along the road or walks in the outskirts of the city, to see a ball, somewhat above the average size of a boy's marble, roll along, while there is no boy in the immediate neighborhood. Sometimes there will be a number of these little balls moving up hill without any apparent propelling power, and in violation of all the laws of force and gravitation. Upon careful examination the foreigner will find a black beetle on the windward side of each ball, standing on its head and hands, and with its hind legs pushing the ball along. This beetle is called, in the vernacular and in Texas, a tumble-bug.

Some scientists have ascertained that the male tumble-bug rolls the balls about for exercise or amusement, just as the fashionable young men push billiard balls about with the cue. Other scientists, however, assert that this is all humbug—that it is only the female tumble-bug that rolls the balls, and that she lays her eggs in them. We do not believe that any female 121 tumble-bug would be so indelicate as to stand on her hands and push a ball along with her feet, as depicted by our artist. It is a slander on the sex. At the same time, as both male and female dress alike—in black— it is a very difficult question to determine.

We have only been acquainted with the tumble-bug during the summer months, and therefore do not know what he does in winter. During the long summer days, however, he is surcharged with industry in the matter of building spheres of the aromatic fertilizer that, either owing to its cohesiveness, or for some other reason, is always chosen, and after having constructed the balls he exhibits more zeal than judgment in rolling them along over every object that intervenes between the place of construction and the hole prepared for them. Standing on his head like a clown in a circus, and placing his hind feet on the ball, he pushes it before, or, more correctly speaking, behind him. He resembles the soldiers who, during the war, preferred to advance backwards, and in the matter of the muscular development of his hind legs, he is related to the mule.

The tumble-bug's wife lays an egg inside the ball, or rather lays an egg and then has the male bug build a ball around it. When finished, he starts out with it, and often makes a hundred futile attempts to get it over an obstruction in his path before he realizes that it would be easier to go around the obstruction. When a tumble-bug gets tired and discouraged trying to roll a ball over rough ground, he quits it right there, but as soon as he is rested he starts another ball in some other locality. That seems to be his mission, just as some men travel about, starting a newspaper, and af-

ter they have rolled it for a while until they get tired,
122 they quit, fly away and start a fresh paper in some
other locality. By the way, there is, or was, a newspaper in Texas called the *Moving Ball*.

Occasionally when he gets his ball in the deep track
of a wheel, he has to roll it along for half a mile before he finds a place to get it out. When a tumble-bug
gets killed by the wheel of a passing vehicle, and
his relatives come out to look for the body, the most
influential member of the family usually, without ad-
ministering on the estate, takes possession of the
property belonging to the deceased, and appropriates
it to his own use and benefit. Quarrels among the bereaved relatives and bitter feuds are often the result
of such proceedings.

Most of the good qualities of the tumble-bug are of
a negative character. He attends strictly to his own
business affairs, and never becomes annoying with a
long bill, which is higher praise than can be truthful-
ly bestowed on the mosquito. The tumble-bug does not
sing, neither does it play on the flute nor piano. The
bug is never guilty of the impropriety of getting into
bed with people, as do fleas and some other insects.
There is another thing about tumble-bugs worthy of
notice. They are all as black as the ace of spades. Nobody ever saw a saddle-colored, cream-colored, or a
mulatto tumble-bug of any color. This speaks whole
volumes in their favor.

THROWING THE LASSO

A rope, or lasso, is a harmless looking thing, but in the hands of a Mexican it becomes a terrible weapon. A Mexican can yank a Yankee, or any other hostile intruder he has a spite at, out of the saddle, as quick as the President of the United States can remove an unworthy office holder who is irregular in sending in his campaign assessments according to the civil service reform rules. The dexterity of a Mexican vaquero in handling a rope has to be seen to be believed. During the war with the French, one of Maximillian's best cavalry officers, a Pole, was caught out, so to speak, by the Mexicans, with a lasso, around Monterey and his neck, and dragged to death. Every Mexican is dangerous when he has got a lasso in his hands. Even a good-natured

Mexican, who has been born without any arms, is not
124 to be trusted when he has got a lasso in his hands—as
we heard an Irishman once remark. In roping cattle
and horses, the Mexican removes the calico remnant
from the shrubbery. A vaquero gracefully swings the
lasso, gives it an apparently careless toss, and it is
sure to encircle the neck of any particular animal in
the herd he may have singled out. He, the Mexican,
then throws his horse on its haunches, the lasso becomes taut, and so does the animal. It is taught that
it is no use trying to escape from a Mexican with a
lasso. Like most other harmless looking weapons, the
lasso is dangerous to persons who do not know how
to handle it, and to demonstrate this we submit the
following:

A few days ago, we met a newly arrived Englishman coming down Austin Avenue on crutches. He
wore his head in a bandage, his nose was skinned,
and there were other indications of his having either
leaned up against the propeller of a mule to rest himself, or of his having questioned the veracity of some
native Texan. When you see an Englishman in Texas,
who looks as if he needed medicine, you may be sure
he is one of Dr. Kingsbury's patients. At least, that
is what all sick Englishmen in Texas claim. This one
told a touching story of how he met Dr. Kingsbury in
London, and after they " 'ad 'ad some 'arf and 'arf, ye
know," the doctor had given him a florid description
of Texas, how pine apples grew on the prickly pear
bushes, and boxes of oranges dropping ripe from the
trees encumbered the sidewalks; but what induced
the young Englishman to leave his happy home and
come to Texas, to enjoy sport and to acquire great
riches, suddenly, was the description of what sport it
was to lasso cattle.

"So you have been roping cattle, have you?" we asked.

He said he had hired a horse, saddle, and "lassoo," and had ridden up to a steer. As his bad luck would have it, he succeeded in throwing the rope over the animal's horns. It galloped off. Johnny followed the doctor's directions about reining in his horse, and the consequence was that the saddle, with the Englishman in it, went over the horse's neck. He had tied the "lassoo" to the pommel of the saddle, just as Kingsbury told him to do. The steer galloped off with the saddle, like a dog with a tin kettle tied to his tail. It was worth $15, which the Englishman had to pay, but as the "lassoo" was gone, too, he paid up cheerfully. He wanted to return to England to write a book about Texas sports and games. He had already written a letter to the London Times denouncing Kingsbury as unreliable. He also wanted the money returned that he had invested in his Texas pleasure trip.

We told him there was no trouble about getting his money. All he had to do was to make out his bill, go over to San Antonio, and present it to Colonel H. B. Andrews, who would hand out a check for the amount; that Col. Peirce, President of the Sunset route, had given Col. Andrews written permission to pay out of his, Andrews' own pocket, any and all sums of money that he pleased to give to dissatisfied English immigrants. The Englishman called a hack to take him to the train bound for San Antonio, and as he disappeared from sight, who should come up but Bill Snort, of the Crosby County *Clarion and Farmers' Vindicator?*

We told Bill about the bad luck of the young Englishman who succeeded in roping a Texan steer, when he, Colonel Snort, spoke up, and said that if he

was properly encouraged he would give us some of
126 his experiences with the lasso.

After having been encouraged twice, with a cigar
thrown in, Bill settled himself in one of the editorial
thrones, and let himself out as follows:

"The first time I ever fooled with a lasso, or rather
got fooled by a lasso, was when I was a mere boy, a
playful child, so to speak. As I did not want to put my
parents to the expense of buying a lasso, I cut twenty
feet off the clothes line. I then took a position on the
corner and lay in wait for a victim. An aged Mexican
came jogging along on a pacing pony, little imagining
what was in store for him. I was nearly delirious with
joy at my lasso catching his horse by the hind foot. As
I had tied the other end of the rope to my wrist, there
was no chance for him to escape. The next thing I
remembered was a jerk at my arm that can only be
compared to the shake of a candidate's hand on election day, after which I trotted mechanically behind
the old Mexican, who did not seem to know what a
smart boy he had caught. The people on the sidewalk
took in the situation, but they were doubled up too
much with laughter to render me much assistance.
When the old Mexican traveled faster I humored him,
and kept up with the procession. I prayed, however,
loud and earnestly, that he might stop before my arm
came off. My prayers were answered miraculous-
ly. He saw what was the matter. He dismounted and
took the rope off his horse's hind leg. Then he began to haul me in as if I were a big fish. I began to
regret that my prayers for him to stop had been so
promptly answered, for there was an expression in
the aged Aztec's collection of features that filled me
with gloomy forebodings. He was not in a hurry to
take the rope oft my wrist. He swung the other end of

the rope around his head, and then I began to revolve around him like a planet around the sun, he keeping up the centrifugal force and the heat with the end of the rope. After he had taken more exercise than was necessary for a man of his age, he took the rope off my wrist, and I flew off into space at a tangent and a high rate of speed. He did not give me back the rope either, but I did not miss it, for I got some more rope at home—got it on the same place, too—when my immediate ancestors discovered that the clothes-line was too short."

"That cured the dog of sucking eggs, didn't it?" queried one of the Sifters.

"Well, my recollection is that it did for a while," resumed Bill, "but the cure was not permanent. About a year afterwards the city marshal issued a proclamation offering twenty-five cents reward for every unlicensed dog delivered at the pound. Here was a chance for a live, energetic boy to turn an honest quarter. The recollection of my former misfortune had faded out with the marks of the rope. I got another lasso, and watched for a dog. The first dog I saw was several sizes too large to suit me, and, besides, I was afraid he would not lead well. With my usual good luck the rope caught him around the neck, and I began to tow him in the direction of the pound. At first he did not understand what I wanted, and held back until I had nearly pulled his head off, when he suddenly came toward me, whereupon I abruptly sat down on the back of my head, and came very near impairing my future usefulness. But that was a splendid dog to lead. He not only came right up to me, but he went past me. The only fault I could find with him was that in passing me he carried off some of my clothes in his mouth. He must have got a taste of me in his mouth, too. He went on past to the end of the rope. This time, 128 fortunately, I had not tied the rope to my wrist, so I did not have to follow him unless I had wanted to. I thought I would check him up a little, so I pulled the rope. I never saw such an easy dog to lead. He turned right around and came back at me with his mouth open, as if he wanted the rest of my clothes and another mouthful of boy. I turned the brute loose, and fled. It was so easy to lead him. I led him right up to a tree, and the affectionate brute would have followed me up the tree if he had only had a ladder. Finally he went off with my lasso, and the two bits I was to get for leading him to the pound. Right then and there, sitting on the limb of that tree, I registered a solemn vow never to fool with a lasso again. But I must be going. I have an appointment. Goodbye."

Death stares old '81 in the face. Its days are numbered and its last hour is at hand. Its ebb of life is low, and the death-rattle can almost be heard as, with one foot already in the grave, it is rapidly hastening into the ultimo of time. A few more hours and all that will be left to remind us of '81 will be some old familiar unpaid bills, and the shattered fragments of the high resolves we made when the year was young. As the old year, shrouded in penitence, regrets and remorse, is salted away in the grave of the past, and the new year, just freed from the womb of futurity, is being dressed in the garments of hope and good resolutions, it is a fitting time to moralize, to hold a convention of one's self, call for an annual report, read and discuss it, and pass resolutions regarding future actions. It is also a good time to take another "last snifter" before swearing off.

Taking a retrospective glance over the late lamented, we find that we have done many things we ought not to have done, and have left undone many things that we ought to have done. We remember one case wherein we failed to do our duty, and for our neglect we can never forgive ourselves. It was on a bright summer morning, some months ago, that a poor but dishonest looking man came slowly up the stairs and, falling over a cast iron waste basket into our editorial boudoir, introduced himself as "An old subscriber." (*Siftings* was only two months old at the time.) He said he did not know how we were able to bear up under the strain of originating so many different things every week, and he just called to help us out by presenting us with an entirely original joke of his own manufacture. He said we could palm it off on the public as our own, without any extra charge. We read the manuscript, and discovered that the joke was one imported by Stephen F. Austin, with the first colonists who came to Texas in 1821, and that it had been in use so much since that it was frayed on the edges, arid needed re-japanning and varnishing to make it look even second handed. Then we took that guileless

man and, after hitting him on the head with an un-
130 abridged Webster's dictionary, threw him out of the
window.

We have ever since been haunted by the thought
that we did not do what was right by that poor, mis-
guided man. We should have taken him out and held
him on the street car track until an Avenue car had
passed over his neck, or we should have compelled him
to smoke one of the five cent cigars out of the box
presented to us by an admirer in Dallas.

We are burdened with self-reproach for having
made many such mistakes, during the year, but—

> *What is done cannot be now amended,*
> *Men will deal unadvisedly sometimes,*
> *Which after hours give leisure to repent.*

After all, however, we have not much cause to com-
plain of the experience, pleasure and profit that 1881
brought us. We feel kindly toward the old year as it
rolls back into the crypt of past ages. Its early days
found us enjoying many blessings, and its close leaves
us in the enjoyment of many more. As the bells "ring
out the old and ring in the new," we sigh over the
Has Been, and turn with a smile of hope and pleasant
anticipations toward the To Be, for—

> *The years have linings, just as goblets do;*
> *The old year is the lining of the new;—*
> *Filled with the wine of precious memories,*
> *The golden Was doth line the silver Is.*

WE HAVE SWORN OFF

On the 1st day of January, 1882, a business meeting of the Proprietors, Editors, and Sifters of this paper was held in the editorial arena at No. 914 Congress Avenue, Austin, Texas. The Proprietors, Editors, and Sifters were all present. In other words we were both in attendance. Judge Sweet and Col. Knox were both put in nomination for the position of chairman. The ballot resulted in a tie vote, each nominee having voted for himself. The deadlock was broken by a motion to elect two chairmen, one to act as presiding officer, while the other should have the floor; motion carried. The reading of the minutes of the last meeting were dispensed with, as there had not been any last meeting.

Judge Sweet presented the following resolution:

WHEREAS, this being the dawn of a new year, and it being right and proper that we celebrate it as has been the custom from time immemorial, therefore be it *Resolved*, THAT WE SWEAR OFF.

The resolution having been adopted, Col. Knox was
132 appointed a committee to draw up a select assortment
of resolutions regarding a swearing off platform.
The Colonel retired, and, after an absence of half an
hour, returned accompanied by the aroma of a coffee
bean, and presented the following:

SIFTINGS' PLATFORM FOR 1882.

Be it Resolved, That during the year 1882 we shall
continue to be, in politics, independent; in criticism,
impartial; in the matter of publishing original poetry, abstemious; in comments, good natured, and in all
things as truthful as heretofore. As our circulation
bids fair to reach 50,000 copies before the end of the
year, we can afford to be magnanimous to our enemies, and therefore promise not to speak of any of
our contemporaries as "hell-hounds." We shall culti-
vate charity and benevolence toward the needy. As
evidence of our intention to relieve the wants of those
less fortunate or less prosperous than ourselves, we
hereby pledge ourselves, on application from any poor
or dishonest person, who will prove to us that he or
she is really deserving of our bounty, to give said person one copy of *Texas Siftings* every week for one
year on receipt of $2 cash, (clubs of five, 25 per cent.
discount. Money to be sent by P. O. orders or in registered letters.)

Resolved, That we shall not refuse any presents (razorback hogs and other livestock excepted) that may
be forced upon us by friends and admirers, and our
public acknowledgment of the same, and our deep
sense of obligation, will be governed by the following
scale: When we receive a present of a hat (our size is
7½), same to be acknowledged in ten lines, and donor
called Major.

When a box of cigars (we smoke Colorado-Maduro) is sent us, a fifteen line acknowledgment, and donor *133* to be called our public-spirited fellow citizen, Colonel ____. Should liquid encouragement accompany the cigars, the donor to receive further military promotion, and to be called a patron of literature; and a touching reference to be made to the disinterested benevolence of his character.

A bottle of home-made mustang wine will only be acknowledged in the advertising columns at usual rates.

Resolved, That we hereby swear off using any stimulating beverages, said swear-off to continue and be in force for one year from date, with the following exceptions regarding time and place, that is to say, that the rules may be suspended, and we may, under advisement, take certain stimulants solely and strictly as medicine:

1. When samples are sent to the office.
2. When laboring under a sense of discouragement.
3. When we receive a new subscriber.
4. When we feel that we actually need something.
5. On any special occasion.

But at all other times we will abstain from drinking anything of a stimulating nature, and, moreover, we solemnly pledge ourselves not to drink anything either during the year 1881, which has just closed, or during any of the previous years since the creation of the world.

Blind Tom plays 7,000 pieces on the piano. He is accompanied by a kind-hearted man who sees that nobody else takes advantage of Tom.

THE EGOTISTICAL BORE

The egotistical bore is quite common, and he is to be found in every grade of society. He never asks your opinion about anything, but, in an I-am-sir-oracle way, says "I feel"—"I am positive that"—"I tell you, sir—" "I can assure you," etc. He utters the most commonplace truisms as if they were original thoughts just coined in his own mental mint, and stamped with his great "I" trademark. He will gravely tell you how you should conduct your business, and he does it with such an air of conscious superiority that you can not decide whether to laugh at him or kick him off the premises. The egotist is always a critic, and to "damn with faint praise" is his forte. "Yes, yes," he will say, "very well done, indeed; very good for a man of his caliber," and then he strokes his upper lip and looks up at the ceiling in a way that says, as plainly as words could, "Lord bless you, you should see how I could do that."

An egotist is always selfish, and does a large business on a very small capital by borrowing, and by exhibiting as cases of genuine goods, what are only empty boxes. Some first class egotists only use two fingers when shaking hands, but the most exasperating characteristic is that, in conversation—if a one-sided interview can be called conversation—a bore of this class pays no heed to what you say, and when he pauses and you, thinking he has finished, start in on your innings, he interrupts you by resuming at the word he left off. You may continue and raise your voice, but that does not stop him. When he does give you a chance to reply, you can see that he is not pay- *135* ing attention to what you have been saying. While you were talking, he was thinking of what he would say when you got through.

A wonderful thing about the egotist is that he never realizes that he is an egotist, and he will talk to you about the evidences of egotism in a mutual friend, and express regret that an otherwise good man should be so afflicted.

Some egotists are amusing, some exasperating, and some should be spread out at the bottom of a deep hole and have railroad iron piled on top of them.

If all the egotists in the world were shot at, very few of us would escape being at least winged by a spent ball.

A FOILED BOOK AGENT

A young man with a large book under his arm and a seven-by-nine smile on his mug stuck his head into the ticket window at the Union depot, and asked the clerk what the fare was to San Antonio.

"Ten dollars and fifteen cents," replied the ticket slinger.

"I am pining to leave Austin, but I lack ten dollars of the ticket money. However, that shan't part us. I'll make a partial cash payment of fifteen cents and take the rest out in trade."

"What do you mean by taking it out in trade?"

"I am a book agent, and if you will let me have the ticket, I won't try to sell you a book. I won't say book to you once. This is the most liberal and advantageous

offer ever made to the public, and you ought to take
136 advantage of it. I have been known to talk a sane
man so completely out of his senses in fifteen minutes
that he wasn't even fit to send to the legislature afterward."

"What book have you got?" asked the ticket agent.

A beaming smile came over the book agent's face,
and in a sing song voice he began:

"I am offering in seventeen volumes Dr. Whiffle-
tree's Observations in Palestine, a book that should
be in every family, a book that comprises the views
of the intelligent doctor on what he saw in the Holy
Land, with numerous speculations and theories on
what he did not see, altogether forming a complete
library of deep research, pure theology and chaste
imagery. I am now offering this invaluable encyclope-
dia for the unprecedented low price of two dollars a
volume, which is really giving it away for nothing—"

After the book agent had kept this up for about ten
minutes, he began to grow discouraged, for, instead
of showing signs of weakening, the ticket agent,
with an ecstatic smile on his face, begged the eloquent man to keep on.

The book agent stopped to rest his jaw when the
ticket man reached out his hand and said: "Shake, ole
fel!" Come inside and take a chair, and sing that all
over again. That cheers me up like a cocktail. I used
to be a book agent myself before I reformed and went
into the railroad business, and that is like music to me.
It soothes me all over. It calls back hallowed memories
of the past, and makes me want to go out on the road
again. I would rather pay twenty dollars than have
you leave Austin. You must come around every day. I
could listen to that all day, and cry for more."

The book agent shut his book and said:

"Some infernal hyena has given me away, but there is another railroad that I can get out of this one- horse town on. I'll not consent to travel on any road that don't employ gentlemen who can treat a cash customer with common politeness. You can't capture my book on any terms, and if you will come out of your cage I'll punch your head in less time than you can punch a ticket." And he passed away like a beautiful dream.

"Do you mean to call me a liar?" asked one rival railroad man of another railroad man, during a dispute on business they had on Austin Avenue yesterday.

"No, Colonel, I don't mean to call you a liar. On the contrary, I say you are the only man in town who tells the truth all the time, but I'm offering a reward of twenty-five dollars and a chromo to any other man who will say he believes me when I say you never lie," was the response.

"Well, I'm glad you took it back," replied the other party, as they shook.

A POETIC GEM

In these days of aestheticism and ultra refinement, a false standard of what constitutes true poetry has been established, and the grandiloquent and turgid style is all the fashion. The so-called poetry of today is made up of equal parts of high sounding words, florid figures, tortuous tropes, and misty metaphors. Let any rhymster select a lofty theme that he does not understand, let him rave and rhyme on that theme in such a manner that his readers will not know whether he is writing about one of the mythological gods or about the death of a mule, and he will be ranked among the poets as long as rhymed bathos will continue to flow out of him.

This vitiated taste for the gaudy, and lurid style of poetry is much to be deprecated, because it blinds its admirers to the beauty of real poetry. It is said to be a fact that traveling men who eat maple syrup, made of glucose and molasses, at hotels and railroad eating houses, at length acquire a taste for it, and actually use it, as a battercake lubricator, in preference to the genuine juice of the maple. So it is in the matter of a *139* taste for poetry, that when the reading and study of the aesthetic school has progressed a certain length, the appreciation of the beauties of genuine poetry is gone for—ever, and there is little hope of reform. The infatuation of its devotees for what is artificial cannot be shaken off.

Before it is everlastingly too late we want to reason with some of the erring ones who admire the glucose kind of poetry like this:

> *Oh, sweet is the whang of the wanglewane,*
> *And the snore of the snark in the twilight pale,*
> *As the krail crawl up the window pane—*
> *(Love me, love, in the grewsome gale.)*
>
> *Gone is the wanglewane, weird and wold,*
> *Down to the gate of the nether land,*
> *Where the horn-toads glide, and the musty mold*
> *Eats the lily in my lost love's hand.*

We want to appeal to their reason, and by presenting an example of true classic poetry, and by pointing out its simplicity and beauty, convince them that they have been following mere bubbles while pearls lay neglected all around them.

It is also our pleasing duty in this connection to rescue from obscurity a poetic gem, the inimitable production of an anonymous genius, who uses words that all can understand. It is no grand epic, no sentimental idyll, no heroic verse, but merely a terse recital of a common incident in ordinary life.

The bard has chosen the narrative style as that most suited to his theme. In the opening line he introduces the principal character in the poem:

There was an old woman who lived in a shoe.

He does not waste time and words invoking the muse, but, with a boldness that is as refreshing and original as it is startling, dashes right into his subject. He does not strive to heighten the interest in his narrative by selecting, as a subject, one of the legendary heroes of antiquity or a heroine of romance, but in terse and perspicuous language he affirms that the central figure in the poem is an "old woman," and there is no circumlocution in his statement as to the humble and quaint shelter in which she was domiciled-" She lived in a shoe." There is no unnecessary verbiage in the line quoted. It reads like a prepaid telegram, yet its euphonism is heightened and its elegance intensified by its brevity.

The fastidious critic may see no beauty in an ancient female, and will doubtless cavil at the selection of such a commonplace heroine, but the impartial student will realize that genius can ennoble the commonest and most uninteresting personage, and throw a halo of romance around even an old woman.

In the second line the poet opens up to us a long vista of possibilities and probabilities. He outlines, or rather hints, at some of the cares of life that have fallen to the lot of this heroine when he tells us that

She had so many children she didn't know what to do.

True art in poetry is to leave to the imagination of the reader the filling up of the picture, to let him surmise the little details incident to the plot, but not necessary to be expressed to make the narrative understood. A bungling tyro would have told us

the ages of the children, and would have discussed their peculiar idiosyncrasies of character. He would *141* probably have introduced the father of the children, a character that would really detract from, rather than add interest to, the pathetic narrative. Our poet, with keen appreciation of literary art, does none of these things, but when he has prepared our minds by the lofty sublimity of the first line, he appeals to our 'sympathies in the second, where he shows how this poor but proud woman was harassed with doubt as to "what to do." We say she was proud, because the poet, with subtle ingenuity, indicated that she was both proud and independent, when he made the simple statement that she had taken up her residence in a shoe. She evidently preferred independence, in the contracted and comfortless confines of an old brogan, to dependence in the gilded halls on the poor farm.

In the next line the character of this true woman and noble mother begins to develop:

She gave them some broth without any bread.

Here the natural instincts of the mother are shown forth in this act of supplying her children with nourishment. She, as we were told, did not know what to do, yet, even under these circumstances she was equal to the occasion, and the grand maternal care of the woman is feelingly portrayed in the evidences of love (and the broth) that she gave her offspring. The broth was without any bread. We are left in a state of delicious uncertainty as to whether it was Scotch broth, chicken broth, or beef broth; but that is an unimportant matter. There is, however, no question as to the bread; there was no bread. The superficial reader might suppose that the fact was mentioned to show the poverty of the woman, and to demonstrate that

she was destitute of the staff of life. That was not the
142 intention of the poet. Through this wise woman's act, and in these seemingly commonplace words, is taught a grand hygienic lesson.

At the hour when the broth was placed before the children, as the concluding lines of this sublime poem evidences, it was night, it was the time when the active body and mind seek needed repose, and when it would have been injurious to the digestive organs of children to have loaded their stomachs with bread, while such an ill-advised course would have, possibly, caused nightmare. The thoughtless may sneer at the heroine's common surroundings, and jest about the plebeian character of her humble abode, but none dare say that she was not in the possession of a level head; and when we come to the concluding lines of this immortal story of a woman's suffering, a woman's patience, and a woman's firmness, we see the veneration for sacred precepts that prompted the last recorded act of this Spartan-like mother—

She whipped them all soundly
and sent them to bed.

Doubtless she disliked to whip them, but she shrank not from the nightly whipping that she considered it her duty to administer. This is an overpowering evidence of the firmness of her character. She not only felt that sparing the rod would spoil the child, but that in the case of children a properly administered castigation is conducive to sleep.

We trust that by calling attention to the grandeur and simplicity of this great poem—grand and simple not only in sentiment, but in construction-we have done something toward reviving a taste for true poetry.

"Do you ever take anything?" asked an Austin candidate, leading a prominent citizen into a saloon.

"Do I ever take anything? Don't you remember I have been a member of the Legislature?"

That settled it. He took something.

A FAIR PROPOSITION

A man was brought up before an Austin justice of the peace, charged with trying to pass a lead counterfeit half dollar.

"What do you mean by trying to palm off such a miserable counterfeit as that on the intelligent people of this University city?"

The prisoner said he didn't mean anything.

"That will not go down with this court. You might have got a better counterfeit than that. How could you expect to deceive the public with that sort of a coin? If I couldn't get up a better counterfeit than that I would be ashamed of myself."

"Well, judge," said the counterfeiter, "I am a businessman, and if you have any better counterfeit than that half dollar, show me your samples, and if the price suits, I'll buy all of my counterfeit money from you. If you don't like that, I'll go in with you on shares."

Judicial indignation, and the committal followed.

TEXAS SOLDIERS

The old-fashioned, brass-mounted Texas soldier, who perished in the Alamo, and who but a short time afterwards made it so hot for the Mexicans at San Jacinto that they wished they had never been born, was a different looking son of Mars from the modern Mardi Gras or Fourth of July soldier. The former was always watching to see a Mexican or an Indian, while the latter is anxious to be seen by the ladies.

In some respect the modern Texas soldier is better off than those who fought during the Texan revolution. A modern Texas soldier is not expected to lay down his life in A. D. 1835 at the Alamo, as did the heroes of that place. He is not supposed to go back *145* forty-six years and overwork himself "removing" Mexicans on the plains of San Jacinto. If the modern Texas soldier needs any exercise he goes out collecting bills, as he is usually a clerk as well as a son of Mars. The modern soldier does not have to march for days and days in the hot sun without any umbrella, and without coming to any place where he can get beer on ice. If the modern soldier wants to go to San Antonio, all he has to do is get on the cars, tell the conductor he represents *Texas Siftings*, and he will arrive there safe and sound, and fresh as a daisy. He gets in the 'bus, is driven to a hotel, where he can have a nice time. If a Mexican gets after the modern soldier in San Antonio, the latter calls for a policeman, and has Mr. Mex. locked up.

That's not the way it was when Texas soldiers made excursions to San Antonio about 1836. They had to walk or ride the whole way. When they got there they were cordially received with grape shot, etc. If they wanted to get into a house, they had to dig their way in with a crow-bar, and kill about forty Mexicans before they would let them alone. That is where the modern Texas soldier has a soft thing of it.

In some other respects the soldier of today has to suffer. Every Mardi Gras there is trouble at Galveston, and he has to go there to see about it. Not long since there was a break-down on the train, and for several hours a whole company of warriors had to fight off the attacks of savage mosquitoes. The enemy never let up, but there was not even a whisper of surrender, although every soldier lost more or less blood. On another occasion a company of modern soldiers captured a breakfast at an eating house at a

railroad station. Every soldier received three or four
146 biscuits in his stomach, and suffered untold agonies
from indigestion, so really the modern soldier has to
suffer as much as did the old-fashioned brass mount-
ed Texans.

By examining the illustration at the head of this
article the intelligent reader will be able to tell which
is which. The soldier with the bouquet in the muzzle
of his gun is the new-fashioned soldier, while the one
with a Bowie knife in his boot, and a slouch hat, is the
sort who used to die at the Alamo, offer up Mexicans
at San Jacinto, and draw black beans as cheerfully as
if they were engaged in celebrating Mardi Gras, or
destroying lunch on the Fourth of July.

A little colored girl applied at the house of a prominent citizen of Austin for a position to wash dishes, etc.

"Where does your mother live?" asked the lady of the house.

"She libs out on Robinson Hill."

"Have you got any father?"

"Yes, ma'am, but he has gone out into de country to pick cotton, but my mudder tole me if I was a good girl, and behaved myself, she would get me a step-fodder until de cotton pickin' season was over."

THE GLORIOUSLY DRUNK MAN

There are a variety of styles and patterns of drunk men, all of them more or less absurd and disagreeable. There is the glorious, the stupid, the pugnacious, the confidential, the weeping, the loquacious, and the morose drunk man, besides many other minor varieties. In this article we shall confine ourselves to the man who gets gloriously drunk.

He is the least objectionable of all the men who get drunk. He is usually a man of generous impulses, broad and liberal views, sanguine temperament, warm hearted and sociable. The miserly, mean, stingy, or small souled men are seldom seen gloriously drunk.

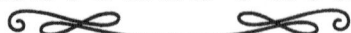

148 Either because they lack enterprise or because they dread the expense consequent on a glorious drunk, they confine themselves to solitary and economical tippling from a bottle that they keep on the upper shelf in the closet at home. You can never tell by looking at a man, when he is sober, what kind of a drunk man he would develop into, if he had the opportunity and the requisite intoxicants, but you can be pretty sure that the niggard, or the man who changes a dime on Sunday morning that he may have a nickel to put in the poor box, never invests in a glorious drunk.

The man who becomes gloriously drunk is usually ripe between 1 and 3 o'clock a.m., when, if he is not harvested by his friends and a hackman, he is liable to be pulled by the police. He takes more enjoyment out of a drunk than any of the other varieties of bacchanalian revelers. His views of life broaden out and his contempt for the details and trivial worries of business strengthen as he warms up under the influence of successive glasses of his favorite beverage. If clouds of adversity or trouble have filled the horizon of his everyday life, these clouds glow with rose tints or disappear altogether before the deceptive influence of the golden liquid as he sucks it through a straw, and tells the barkeeper to "charge 'em to me." He "sets 'em up" with a munificent liberality, not only to his friends, but to any chance acquaintance, or even strangers, that may be in the saloon.

As he warms up he is apt to break forth into song. His favorite selections are of the "Drive-dull-care-away" and "Won't-go-home-till-morning" class, and he is extremely partial to anything with a Hip, Hip, Hurrah! chorus to it. When he reaches the musical period of his drunk, he usually has his hat on one side of his head and mud on his coat tail.

The man who gets gloriously drunk never does anything by halves. He is sure to get gloriously sick *149* next morning. He is not an habitual drunkard (the latter never gets glorious), but merely once in a while, without premeditation, he meets a couple of friends whom he has not seen for some time, the temptation—and the liquor—is too strong, and the result, next morning, is a headache, brandy and soda, and a determination never to do so any more. His two friends usually belong to the royally drunk and the boisterously drunk class.

WHY PARSON CAME TO TEXAS

A good many years ago, when Austin was a very small town, quite a number of prominent citizens went out on a hunting expedition. One night when they were all gathered around the camp fire, one of the party suggested that each man should give the time and reason for his leaving his native State and coming to Texas, whereupon each one in turn told his experience. Judge Blank had killed a man in self-defense, and Arkansaw. Gen. Soandso had forged another man's signature to a check, while another came to Texas on account of his having two wives. The only man who did not make any disclosures was a sanctimonious-looking old man, who, although a professional gambler, was usually called "Parson."

"Well, Parson, why did you leave Kentucky?"

"I don't care to say anything about it. Besides, it was only a trifle. None of you would believe me anyhow."

"Out with it! Did you shoot somebody?"

"No, gentlemen, I did not. But since you want to
150 know so bad, I'll tell you. I left Kentucky because I did
not build a church."

Deep silence fell on the group. No such excuse for
coming to Texas ever had been heard before. There
was evidently an unexplained mystery at the bottom
of it. The "Parson" was called on to furnish more light.

"Well, gentlemen, you see a Methodist congregation raised $3,000 and turned it over to me to build a
church—and I didn't build the church. That's all."

DEATH IN THE POT

From time to time we read of the dreadful poisons
contained in common articles of food, and we are told
of danger and death lurking in the most unexpected
places, and concealed under the most innocent guise.
We become horrified as we realize how, for years and
years, we have been slowly but surely filling our blood
with deadly poisons, ruining our constitution with unhealthy viands, and taking risks that a graveyard
insurance company would shudder to think of. One
paper tells us that there is enough poison contained
in one cigar to kill a dog; in the next family journal
that we pick up, we read that there is more prus-
sic acid in an almond than would extinguish the vital
spark in a mouse, and then comes a note of warning regarding our favorite beverage, coffee; we learn
that sufficient poison can be extracted from a pound
of coffee to poison two men and a boy. As soon as we
have revised our commissary department and begin
to feel safe once more, we are startled by statistics
regarding the number killed annually by the bursting
of millstones, or the unhealthy vapors arising from
stagnant buttermilk.

About a year ago, we had discarded everything that we thought was dangerous, when we were startled on learning that the syrup of commerce was adulterated with nitric acid, and that miasma lurked in the deadly folds of the boarding-house battercake. Figures were given to show that the dreadful battercake habit was spreading, and prophecies were made that it would eventually ruin the constitution of its strongest devotees, and reduce the nation to a vast hospital of flap-jack invalids; so the battercake was scratched off our list of edible fruits, and next went the fragrant codfish ball, because it was said to produce cold feet. Then we learned that the sad-faced and cohesive biscuit was a synonym of indigestion, and the unostentatious kraut but another name for rheumatism, so the biscuit and the kraut had to go; then we found out that castor oil contained the germs of ingostatic molecules, whatever that is, and we were, therefore, forced to give up the use of that hilarious medicinal beverage.

This thing went on until we had cut off everything from our bill of fare but cistern water and chewing gum, and yet we found ourselves no stronger nor healthier than when we were rapidly hastening to the tomb from the effects of gorging ourselves with a heavy line of assorted poisons three or four times a day. About this time, a man came along with a magic lantern and showed us that every drop of cistern water contained an aquarium of hideous marine monsters with wiggling tails, and a druggist told us that the habit of gum chewing was a fruitful source of cancer.

Next thing we did was to swear off being an infernal fool on the diet question; and, now, we eat anything and everything that our teeth will masticate, or our palate commend, and we can work ten hours a day and see to read small print without spectacles.

THE OMNIPOTENT Rope IN TEXAS.

The children cry for it!

The boys play with it!

The young men live by it.

CATTLE THIEF

Some old ones die by it.

THE AWFUL COAL BUG

An entomologist has discovered what he calls the coal bug, or the cimex anthracitus. We have been reading up on the history and habits of the interesting little insect, and it is with mingled feelings that we sit down to record the result of our investigations. Professor Rodagash, of Stockholm, says that the insect may be considered as a descendant of the prehistoric tree bug. Professor Otto Hechelmeyer says: "It is very noticeable that the so-called coal dust is peculiar on account of its round appearance. Upon examination, with the microscope, it is found that these particles are covered with millions of cimex anthracitus."

We learn, further, that each one is about the size of the head of a needle, flat in appearance, and that they are plentiful at the bottom of coal veins, from whence they work their way to the top. The male is of a gray black color, and has six spots on his back. The female is broad, and has nine spots. When the Professor told us that the crackling sound we hear when fresh coal is put on the fire, "is caused by the death struggles of these insects," our soul was filled with gloom and remorse as we thought of the millions of the descendants of the prehistoric tree bug—the gentle cimex anthracitus, that have been sacrificed through our selfish desire to have warm feet. When we thought of this heedless waste of life for our comfort that we had been guilty of, we were bowed down with grief. When we learned that the cooking of a pan of biscuit was the death knell of a million little cimex anthracitus with six, or mayhap nine spots on their backs, and

that what was, to us, the grateful crackling sound
from our thanksgiving turkey as it roasted before 155
the fire, was the requiem—the funeral dirge—of perhaps a hundred million innocent microscopic bugs,
that had never done us any harm, we went down into
the coal cellar and wept over the few remaining cimex anthracitus that were left to us, and we felt as
if we never could burn anything again but green oak
wood; but when we came back, and, continuing our
investigations further, found that Professor Oxfeller
calls the descendants of the prehistoric tree bug "Aw-
ful insects," and says:

> Servant girls, stokers in fire rooms, and house-
> wives cannot be too careful when moving about
> a coal pile, for if one of these minute creatures
> should get upon their clothing or flesh, the
> former would be eaten into holes quicker than
> by moths. When they become attached to the
> skin of a person they burrow in, and, burying
> themselves, multiply fast, producing a white
> swelling, which eventually results in a soft-
> ening of the bones and a horrible death. Coal
> miners who imbibe large quantities of whiskey
> are never attacked by these insects.

When we read this we wiped our tearful eyes, took
something to prevent softening of our bones, and
wrote an order for another ton of cimex anthracitus.

THE COUNTY FAIR

The county fair is one of the oldest institutions of this country. We have traced its growth and progress until we have found its origin almost lost in the mildewed past. Away back in the mists of antiquity, we find records of the first county fair in the United States. The county fair did not exactly come over in the *Mayflower*, but it was perpetuated by the Plymouth Rock people. It was projected by some of the Mayflower passengers soon after their arrival. The facts are as follows—they are historical facts, so we cannot vouch for them:

Some time in Anno Domini 1760, a man, in Maryland, named Sam Johnson, had a pumpkin patch. It was about two acres in extent, and fenced with cedar pickets. We are particular about giving details, because this is history. Johnson's neighbor, a man by the name of Williams—Dick Williams—also had a pumpkin patch. There was only one acre of it, and it had a stake and rider fence around it. Dick owned a brindle dog, named Tyke. We cannot find that the dog ever did anything extraordinary, or cut any figure in the pumpkin imbroglio. We mention him, however, because this is history we are writing, and history is made up of such trifles.

Johnson found a very large pumpkin in the Southeast corner of the patch, and immediately afterwards, Williams discovered a still larger pumpkin in the Northwest corner of his acre of pumpkins. Each of them determined to encourage his pumpkin to beat that of the other. Williams took the *American Agriculturalist*, while Johnson subscribed to a grange paper and Landreth's Almanac. They read up all the authorities on pumpkins, and then put their fruit under a course of treatment. Williams used guano and phosphates on his. Johnson, by sweating, blanketing, and exercise, soon got his pumpkin to about equal in size the berry of his neighbor Williams.

When the pumpkins were about ready to drop from the tree, the respective owners of each swore that his was the best. They were about to quarrel, when Johnson proposed to refer the matter to Deacon Long-Suffering Simpson. The Deacon was unable to decide, and suggested a committee. The committee failed to agree, and called a meeting of all the people of the colony to decide the matter, and forever set at rest the question as to which of the two pumpkins was the best, and the most calculated to promote and advance the interest of the young and struggling colony. The people met, and, after mature deliberation, decided that Williams' pumpkin was the largest and most nutritious, and better suited for all purposes for which pumpkins were intended, but that Johnson's pumpkin was of the short-horned variety, and, fur-

thermore—which was most important—it was raised
158 from imported seed, seed that came from England,
from the hot-house of the Duke of Hereford, Johnson
having the pedigree of the seed in his possession. So
Johnson was declared the victor, and had a blue ribbon
nailed to the masthead of his pumpkin.

This was the origin of the county fair. The neighbors
of Johnson and Williams went to raising pumpkins,
and their wives planted rags and patches and raised
a crop of rag carpets and patchwork quilts, which
they took along with the pumpkins next year for
exhibition. Then the man with the headless rooster
came along, and the gubernatorial candidate was put
on exhibition and made an agricultural address; other
patent windmills were exhibited, and, gradually, the
county fair grew and developed; but it was not until
the patent churn man, the blind foreigner with the
hand organ, and the fellow with the blue and red bal-
loons came to the front, that the county fair became
a permanent institution.

Fairs are instituted and carried on for the encouragement of farmers struggling with overgrown hogs,
calves, and other farm products; also that awards of
merit may be given to all the sewing machine and
piano makers in the country. Of late, horse-races have
been added to the county fair programme. Of course,
only sinful men who wear horseshoe scarf pins, go
to see the races. The superintendents of county fairs,
desirous of catering to the prejudices and tastes of all
classes, have it so arranged that all the good respectable taxpayers and church members can go over to
the cattle sheds and watch the Durham cows chew
their cuds, while the races are going on. To stand and
look at a cow chewing her cud has always an exhila-
rating effect on us. We like the excitement of it, but,

somehow, when we attend county fairs we are invariably caught in a crowd, just in front of the race track *159* when the races are taking place, and cannot get out until the race is over. This is very embarrassing, and but we are getting away from the historical aspect of the county fair, and will, therefore, stop.

THE UNHAPPY FARMER

There are very few people, excepting perhaps dead people, or those who have never been born, who are quite satisfied with their lot in life. The merchant complains of overwork if he has too much business, and he is far from being perfectly happy if he has no business at all. The doctor, the lawyer, in fact, almost everybody, grumbles more or less under the most favorable or unfavorable circumstances. We grumble from the cradle to the grave, and there are some people who will not be happy in Heaven, if they are not allowed to grumble. We have read of a sick boy, who grumbled because his mother did not put as big, or as hot a mustard plaster on him as she did on his less deserving brother. The professional patriot is always predicting that the country is rapidly going to the dogs, but somehow the country never manages to catch up with the dog. But for solid, unremitting grumbling, the farmer has no equal.

He begins early in the spring and he never takes a vacation. When he comes to town he wears such a sad expression, that his city friends ask him if he has come to town for a coffin. He replies that he might as well get one to fit himself, for all the indications are, that there will be a late frost, and if there is, he will starve to death, but he does not care for any coffin.

160 The crops the previous year were too poor to justify his reveling in such luxuries. It is plain to see that if there is no late frost, he will feel that life is but an empty dream. Sure enough the late frost fails to keep its appointment. The growing crops are in a splendid condition, notwithstanding the farmer seeks to discourage them by walking out among the cotton and corn, shaking his head and sighing heavily.

When he comes to town he looks so ill that the undertakers follow him up. When his city friends ask him if he has the toothache, he shakes his head and says, "I might as well have no teeth at all. There will be nothing for them to bite this year. I was afraid that there would be no late frost to kill off the bugs and the grubs. It is just what the young grasshopper wants. When there is no late frost the season is sure to be sickly. I expect to mortgage my farm to buy quinine."

And that is the dirge he keeps on chanting. After a while it becomes very evident that there will be plenty of corn and cotton. That is more than he can bear up under. Once more he lifts up his voice in lamentation, like Jeremiah with the cramp colic. "Corn will be down to thirty cents. It won't pay to haul it to market. I knew from the start this was going to be a bad year on farmers." When he is asked how about the cotton, he groans some more, and says: "I reckon we will raise enough cotton to feed the worms. I hope we won't make a bale to the acre, because it don't do us any good. The merchants get it all. We only raise cotton for the merchants, and the worms. If we can only fill them up, I reckon we ought to be satisfied, and ask Governor Roberts to order thanksgiving services."

There are some farmers, of course, who laugh and take the weather as it comes, but they do not enjoy life as much as those who understand the business.

Gus De Smith came down Austin Avenue yesterday with his chin cut in several places, so that it looked as if a drunken barber had been practicing on it.

"Merciful Heavens, Gus!" exclaimed Gilhooly, "what did you do to the barber? You ought to have murdered him. That was the least you could have done."

"I didn't do anything of the kind. After he was through shaving, I invited him across the street, and treated him to a cocktail and a cigar."

"Well, you are a fool."

"No, I ain't such a fool after all," responded Gus, "for you see I shave myself." ·

"Oh, that's a different thing. You are a kind of double-barrelled fool."

ANOTHER BRASS-
MOUNTED OFFER

As we have before hinted in this paper, the country is full of philanthropists who propose enriching the publishers of newspapers by offering them due bills in payment for advertisements, these due bills to be sent back to the advertiser, accompanied by sums of money ranging from $10 to $50, in lieu of which the advertiser promises to send the publisher either a Stop-action Havana-filler Sewing Machine, a cord of sheet music, a gallon of non-corrosive extra dry Robinson county printer's ink, an automatic cut-off double-cylinder liver pad, or a recipe for taking grease spots and iron mold out of a dog. The financial genius of the business man is shown in these brilliant offers, and his shrewdness in the seductive circular that contains them. The strong point—to the advertiser—in these circulars is, that the money the publisher sends, when he has published the advertisement for the time required, and when he returns the due bill, is more than the actual cost of the *163* article or articles that the advertiser agrees to send to the publisher, the former, therefore, getting his advertisement free of cost. Since we, some time ago, published our views regarding some of the princely offers of the above described character that we received, there has been a marked falling off in the number of gaudy proposals we receive at this office; still there is occasionally one received that, with its visions of wealth and lurid hints of opulence, takes the breath away from our business manager, and causes him to refer it to us. He has just handed us one which he says is deserving of editorial attention.

We find this to be a very exceptional offer, as the party making it does not ask us to pay anything for the privilege of inserting his ad, but actually, strange as it may seem, offers to pay something to have the advertisement published. We will not give the real name of the concern, as that would be giving it a free advertisement. The circular explains itself, and so does our reply, which is appended:

ADVERTISING DEPARTMENT
January 10, 1882

GENTLEMEN:— We hand you proposition to insert advertisement of six inches space (copy herewith) in your paper for twelve months, as per contract enclosed, to be paid in trade as named.

We will give you four boxes of a new brand of Cigars, of good quality, fine color, agreeable taste and flavor, smoke freely, white ashes, and cannot fail to please any editor or person who may want a good cigar for private use. They are neatly packed in boxes of 50 cigars each, bearing special trademark label, as per copy enclosed, and sell for $4.50 per box, the lowest price at which they can be purchased.

In lieu of cigar proposition, we offer to you one case containing twelve quart bottles of O. F. C. Taylor Old 1873 Hand-Made Sour Mash Whiskey, at $18.00, our cash price per case for this article, and two boxes of cigars. In filling out your contract, please erase either the whiskey or the cigars clause, so that we may know your choice and which of the goods to ship to you.

Return advertising contract to us, duly filled out and signed, on receipt of which we will send you the full matter on stereotype plate by mail.

OFFICE OF TEXAS SIFTINGS, AUSTIN.
January 16, 1882

GENTLEMEN:— Your very liberal offer of the 10th inst. to hand.

It is a very tempting proposal, *twelve quarts of whiskey!* Hand-made Sour Mash, too, and Old 1873 at that! What brilliant editorials there would be in those twelve quarts of inspiration, what sublime and refulgent locals, what radiant and glittering obituary notices, and what luminous and soul-stirring dramatic criticisms! and then to think of what a phosphorescent and lambient sheen we could throw over a market report if we only had the encouragement of a single quart of your old sour mash. But alas! it cannot be. There are insurmountable obstacles in the way of accepting your proposition, and, more in sorrow than in anger, we respectfully decline it. *165*

In the first place, as you will see by referring to the 7th of January edition of our paper, we have "sworn off" for the year 1882, and therefore could have no use for your whiskey. Why did you make your offer at such an inopportune time? If you had only waited until February, or even the end of the present month, we might have been in a position to—but no, even then we couldn't, because that matter-of-fact business manager of ours says that, although we may put what we blank please in the editorial columns, he won't put a six inch display in the advertising end of the paper for less than several hundred dollars cash, quarterly in advance.

Now, although we feel that your twelve quarts of sour mash would do us several hundred dollars' worth of good, up here in the editorial room, when we are wrestling with a pun, or fatigued by the labor of manufacturing facts and creating statistics, yet we must give way to that soulless business manager, who charges for everything by the line or inch. We presume, that as soon as we recover from our present swearing off spell, we will have to go back to the old legitimate way of getting our sour mash—by winking at the barman and getting him to put it on the slate.

Although we cannot do business with you just now, we commend the effort you are making to encourage the press and to ameliorate the condition of the journalist. We can fancy that, with the naked ear, we can hear the jubilant howl of the editors all over the land who have accepted your offer, and who, as a consequence, are full of Old 1873 Hand-made Sour Mash. We can imagine that we see their local columns filled with sour mash puffs and typographical errors; and we do not strain our imagination when we picture the enterprising editor taking one of the cigars you recommend "for private use," and stealing off privately, far from the busy haunts of men, to smoke it on the top of some high mountain on a windy day.

Respectfully yours,

SWEET & KNOX

MALARIAL INTOXICATION

In San Antonio and in some other cities, it has been customary, for many years past, to publish weekly mortuary reports for the purpose of informing those inhabitants who are still alive, of the names of those who have died, and what particular disease they died of. In order to bring this information within the reach of all who can read, the Latin and Greek names of the diseases are given. This is an excellent idea If a member of the family dies, it is consoling to the survivors to read in the mortuary report that it was not jaundice, but Icterus acutus febrilis apaticus. Nobody could reasonably expect to survive all that. When a person reads that, he is astonished that the patient did not die sooner and more frequently. Again, it flatters common folks to read that some poor devil has died of a disease with a name a mile and a half long, while in the very same mortuary report perhaps some wealthy banker has been called hence on a dis- *167* ease of only two syllables.

Over in San Antonio, thanks to successive city phy-sicians, the people die of icterus senilis, of seven kinds of tuberculoses; of icterus amenorrhoea, intestinalis pulmonalis, and five other kinds of icterus. They can also die, if they want to, of anenisma, colica flatulenta, biliosa—particularly when complicated with atrapia medullae spinalis or marasmus infantium, caused probably by too much vox populi, nux vomica, e pluri-bus unum, etc., particularly etc.

Of course the people of San Antonio were a little confused at first, to know what diseases they had died of, but at length they tumbled to the racket, and have educated themselves up to the technical terms. Nobody in San Antonio asks, "How is your prickly heat coming on?" Thanks to the city physician's mor-tuary reports, instead of asking, "How is your prickly heat today?" the Alamo citizen asks "How is your eczema solare coming on?" to which the sufferer re-plies, "Much better, thank you. It was not the regular eczema solare at all, but only eczema impetigion oi-des, complicated a little with chloasma ephelis." If the other party does not want to give himself away, he will not ask if that is the barber's itch, for it is not, although it is somewhat similar, being rather in the nature of porrigo lupinosa.

So completely have the San Antonio people educat-ed themselves up to calling things by their proper names that nothing is more common than to hear even colored people conversing somewhat in the fol-lowing style: "I say, Uncle Mose, how's yer chile comin' on? I heered yer was up all night wid it, dat it had de wussest kind ob peretonitis ob de mucus membrane

mi#ed up wid vomitus chronicus, and a misery in de
168 chist." To this Uncle Mose responds, "De chile has
done got ober all dat, but dis mornin' hit was all broke
out wid epilepsia thoracica, but I has strong hopes ob
hits gettin' well ef laryngostenose don't sot in. I's had
a tech myself ob de rheumatismus paralyticus runnin'
up my left leg, but I jess knocked de stiffness out ob
hit wid angle worm oil."

These technical terms may not be correct, but they
answer the purpose just as well as any others.

Not long since, in glancing over the San Antonio papers, we were surprised to read that somebody, for
the first time in many years, had died of an intelligi-
ble malady. It read that: "Mr. Blank, aged 36, malarial
intoxication." Jess so. That's plain enough. Mr. Blank,
while suffering from malaria, tried to cure it with
some of Sam. C. Bennett's sour mash whiskey, and
between the malaria and the remedy, the poor man
failed to survive. It was a great source of satisfaction
for us to know precisely what one person in San Antonio really did die of. It was not too much gastroata#ia
saburralis, or even of haematernesis, of cardia podo-
gracia, or any of those ordinary modes of shuffling
off the mortal coil, but simply malarial intoxication.
Our satisfaction that people over at San Antonio had
returned to the old-fashioned diseases was of short
duration, for the very next day our eye was riveted
in its socket by the following card from Dr. Menger,
the city physician, in the San Antonio *Evening Light*:

SAN ANTONIO, Jan. 25, 1882.

Editors *Evening Light*:

In regard to the term "malarial intoxication,"
as certified in his death certificate, by the attending physician, and in my weekly mortuary

report, I noticed in your yesterday's Light that this appears to be a mistake, and that it should have been "malarial toxicohoemia."

Now allow me to mention that although I was aware of the mistake in the term "intoxication," I still mentioned it in my weekly report because I can only make out a copy of the certificates of deaths issued.

The technical meaning of the term in this case is not "intoxication" nor "toɤicohremia," but "toɤicohremia," from the Greek or Latin "toɤikon" —a poison, and haema—blood; therefore, blood poisoning.

Respectfully,
DR. R. MENGER

FAIR PROPOSITION

A man was brought up before an Austin justice of the peace, charged with trying to pass a lead counterfeit half dollar.

"What do you mean by trying to palm off such a miserable counterfeit as that on the intelligent people of this University city?"

The prisoner said he didn't mean anything.

"That will not go down with this court. You might have got a better counterfeit than that. How could you expect to deceive the public with that sort of a coin? If I couldn't get up a better counterfeit than that I would be ashamed of myself."

"Well, judge," said the counterfeiter, "I am a businessman, and if you have any better counterfeit than that half dollar, show me your samples, and if the price suits, I'll buy all of my counterfeit money from you. If you don't like that, I'll go in with you on shares."

Judicial indignation, and the committal followed.

A YANKEE DESPERADO

I t is very surprising what a big business some men can do on a credit bases, where there is little or no capital invested.

As any of the old inhabitants of San Antonio will remember, about the year 1851, the most influential man in that city was an alleged desperado named Bob Augustine. Bob came to San Antonio with a fearful record. He enjoyed the reputation of having killed a dozen men, and was respected accordingly. While he was in San Antonio he did not reduce the census at all, but that was not his fault. He had a seductive way of drawing his 18-inch Arkansaw tooth-pick, and examining it critically with a sinister smile, while humbly requesting the temporary loan of $5. The people were very kind to him. They took into consideration that he was an influential stranger, and they humored his whims and caprices to the extent of their means. They were anxious that he should not be unfavorably impressed with the people, or that it should not

be said such an influential stranger had been treated
with discourtesy.

Bob did his very best to induce the leading citizens
to furnish him with some incentive to squander their
gore, but in vain. If he asked a rich merchant to exe-
cute the Highland Fling, rather than injure the future
prospects of the place he would do so, and then in-
sist on loaning Bob money without exacting security.
Thus it was that Bob went about acquiring wealth
and warm personal friends, but creating no funerals.
There were some rumors that Bob was playing bluff,
but they originated after he had moved away.

It was during the reign of Bob Augustine, "the long-
ranged Roarer of Calaveras Canyon," as he familiarly
called himself, that a young man, from Boston, named
John Winthrop, came to San Antonio, presumably in
search of health, as he brought very little with him.
He was far gone in consumption, and nothing but the
fact that he had but a short time to live, unless the
climate of Western Texas saved him, induced him to
come to San Antonio. As everybody carried a pistol,
Winthrop did not care to insult public decency by going unarmed. Besides, such a course might as seriously
interfere with his restoration to health as putting on
a clean shirt. His Puritan training caused him to re-
volt at the idea of carrying fire-arms, so he resorted
to artifice. He wore a holster but instead of keeping
a pistol in it, he had his cash funds stored away in
it, and nobody was the wiser for it. On the contrary,
Winthrop was looked up to by the best citizens just
the same as if he was loaded down with deadly weapons.

Of course everybody tried to make the stranger
from Massachusetts feel as comfortable as if he were
at home; so he was told all about Bob Augustine, the

long-ranged roarer, at least ten times a day, and he
172 was advised not to be particular in asking security
for the debt in case the roarer wanted to borrow a
small, temporary loan, unless he, Winthrop, did not
wish to regain his health.

As might have been expected, the long-ranged roarer called on Winthrop to collect his usual assessment
on strangers. Winthrop was of the opinion that if he
saved his life and lost all his money he would be doing unusually well. The long-ranged roarer's idea was
to chase the blue-bellied Yankee around the room a
time or so, collect $5 or $10, and perhaps make some
earmarks, a la Whittaker, so he would know him in a
crowd if he should meet him again.

The long-ranged roarer sauntered into Winthrop's
room at the hotel, but before the desperado could
open his mouth or draw a weapon, the unfortunate
Yankee threw back his coat, and with trembling fingers tugged at his pistol holster to get at his money
to appease the would-be assassin. On the other hand,
as soon as the Roarer saw Winthrop trying to get out
his pistol, he turned as pale as a ghost. The alleged
desperado's knees knocked together; the cold sweat
boiled out all over him, and he extended his hand and
said, in trembling accents:

"Don't draw, good Mr. Yankee! I was only trying to
fool you. My bold Arkansaw heart beats for you, my
boy. I jest wanted to teach you a lesson. Never let any
damed galoot get the drop on you. If anybody insults
you, jest tell them that Bob Augustine, the Roarer, is
your friend."

Winthrop, who was worse scared, if possible, than
the Roarer, replied. "Oh, I'll give you what you want,"
and kept on tugging at the holster, which came un-
buckled.

With a yell of dismay, the desperado passed out through the window, carrying off the sash, and ran *173* down Commerce street, the principal thoroughfare, with the sash on his neck, howling, "Police! Police!" closely pursued by Winthrop, who kept on tugging at his holster, trying to get out his money, he believing that the desperado was running to his room to procure a shotgun with which to commit murder. All that afternoon Winthrop kept on hunting the Roarer to purchase peace on any terms, and the Roarer hid himself to avoid the pistol of the Boston man. Next morning the long-ranged Roarer of the Calaveras Canyon was missing, while Winthrop was the lion of the day for having run off the terror of the Alamo City.

Now for the sequel. Winthrop afterward moved to Galveston, and now is one of the merchant princes of the Island City. Lately, as he was coming down to his place of business, a decrepit old beggar on crutches held out his hand. Col. Winthrop thought he recognized the man, and he asked, "Don't you remember trying to borrow five dollars from me in San Antonio about thirty years ago? Ain't you the long-ranged Roarer of the Calaveras Canyon?"

The aged mendicant gave a look of mortal terror, and tried to run on his crutches, but his old would-be benefactor pressed the five dollars into his hand, and of course there was an affecting scene on the sidewalk.

It has been rumored that the citizens of San Antonio, finding out that Bob Augustine, the Roarer, was a fraud, hung him to a China tree on the military plaza for contempt of court or disorderly conduct.

It was also rumored that Bob Augustine made his escape from San Antonio, reformed, changed his

name, and is now no other than Mr. Moody, the great
174 revivalist.

All these rumors are now definitely set at rest by the fact that the Roarer is now an aged cripple in Galveston, but in very reduced circumstances.

EDITORIAL SERMON

Mr. N. Webster, the author of that popular but desultory volume that all of us turn to for information of an orthographical or exegetical character, defines the word dividend as follows: "A part or share; particularly the share or profit of stock in trade or other employment, which belongs to each proprietor according to his proportion of the stock or capital." Railroad companies, banks, mining companies and other corporations pay dividends at least some of them do. The men to whom the dividends are paid, carry gold-headed canes, live in three-story bricks, dine at 6 p.m., and are usually among the most respectable members of society. They are to be found in all parts of the country, mostly, however, in cities, and besides drawing their dividends, many of them attend to other business, although it is a noteworthy fact that in no instance has any of them ever been found editing a Texas weekly paper or driving a milk cart.

We who dine at noon, live in one-story cottages with mortgages on them, and have wet blankets thrown over us as we slowly elbow our way through life, sometimes envy the old cornucopias as we see them go down to the bank to draw their dividends. We forget that there are dividends and dividends, and that the good lexicographer did not cover the whole ground 175 when he defined the word dividend.

A poor man struggles against poverty, labors hard and economises that he may be able to provide a good education for his son. The son, benefiting by the advantages that his father's self-denial, love, and ambition provide for him, completes his collegiate course, takes a place high among his fellows, and begins his upward and onward course on the ladder of fame. At every successive round that he reaches, a dividend is declared, and who will deny that the latter is the beneficiary "according to his proportion of the stock or capital," as Webster puts it?

A young man obtains a position as assistant in a store or office. He gets a small salary but he gives all his energy and attention to his employer's interest. He tells the truth, and his leisure hours are spent in study that will fit him for a higher position. He does not drink, and he is as ignorant of the tactics of the billiard and card room as the average railroad-office clerk is of the rules of politeness. He acquires reputation for sobriety, energy, honesty, and industry, and when his employer wants a man to fill a position where such qualities will be valuable, this young man is offered the position with the superior emoluments that belong to it—he draws a dividend. Morality, integrity, and industry, the capital invested; reputation and promotion the dividend declared.

A good man gives a helping hand and kindly advice to those whom adversity, or a "weakness" of some kind, has brought low, and he draws his dividend when he learns that his assistance and encouragement have smoothed the pathway and lightened the load of his suffering fellow.

176 The charitable man gives to the poor and the needy of his abundance, and having thus lent to the Lord, he draws a compound-interest dividend in the satisfaction he feels at having done his duty, and the pleasure he experiences when he sees the recipients of his charity fed and clothed and thus better prepared to struggle with the hardships of life.

We could write of the dividends drawn by the lazy man, the man of promise without performance, the dissipated man, and he who wantonly kicks a sleeping dog, but we prefer not to elaborate that side of the picture. For all of us, if we labor honestly, earnestly, and industriously, there are dividends to be drawn, and if, in this world, we do our duty according to our light, and observe the golden rule, we shall, in the land of the leal, draw the greatest dividend of all when we hear the approving: "Well done, thou good and faithful servant."

There was quite a row in the Blue Light Colored Tabernacle night before last, between Uncle Mose and Deacon Gabe Snodgrass.

"You is de biggest black rascal in Austin," said Deacon Snodgrass.

"You is a heap bigger one," responded Uncle Mose, placing his hand on the ivory handle of his umbrella.

"Bredderen," said Parson Bledsoe, "you talks as if dar was nobody present 'ceptin' yerselfs."

THE CHAPARRAL COCK

This elegantly shaped bird, with a long tail and a top-knot, is called by the Americans, the chaparral cock. The Mexicans call him *el caporal,* or the corporal. The American name chaparral cock is evidently the Mexican name *caporal* Americanized. Why the Mexicans call this bird a corporal we do not know, but we can guess. Possibly the Mexicans detect some semblance to a corporal in the top-knot, but our private opinion is that there is another reason for it. Very likely the Mexican corporal is in the habit of getting away from danger faster than the rank and file, and as this bird can run faster than anything else that has legs, the Mexicans, to poke fun at the bird, promoted him to the rank of corporal. This, however, is a mere surmise.

The chaparral cock is such a fast bird, that he makes better time standing still than is made by most railroad trains in Texas. He runs like a Bourbon Democrat in the blue-grass region of Kentucky, but he cannot fly worth a cent. There is really no occasion for his running so fast in order to make a living, as

178 his diet consists exclusively of bugs and insects that crawl on the ground. The chaparral cock is not a shy bird. He stands around and looks at you very much as if he wanted to be invited to take something.

The chaparral cock is not only a handsome bird, but he is very useful. He seems to have been created for the special purpose of preventing centipedes from being too numerous. He patronizes all kinds of bugs, but the centipede gets most of his custom. As soon as a chaparral cock sees a lonesome centipede, he takes up with him, or to be more correct, takes him up. A peculiar feature of the performance is that he does not kill the centipede at once, but picks him up in his bill, and runs about with him. Why the chaparral cock goes through this performance, we do not know. He is not a communicative bird. We can only surmise. It may be that he carries the centipede about in that way in order to amuse himself. Our own impression is that he runs about to get up an appetite. He has too much sense to eat the centipede alive, so, after he is tired furnishing the insect with transportation, he takes him up by the head, and passes him sideways through his bill, very much as a shirt collar is passed through a patent clothes wringer. After this process is completed, the insect has no objections to make to being swallowed, and the sagacious bird gobbles him endways.

The newspapers that are always boasting of having the largest circulation of any paper published in Texas, but are careful never to give any figures, remind one of the poor but proud old lady, who beat a rag with the back of a hatchet every morning, in order to make the neighbors believe she had beefsteak for breakfast.

THE WEEPING
DRUNK MAN

Unlike the gloriously drunk man, whose peculiar characteristics we described in another sketch, the subject of this article seems to take no pleasure out of his drunk. He never makes a night of it, and he is not in the habit of rushing around with his hat on the back of his head, slapping his friends on the back and asking them to come along an d take something. He wears his hat drawn down over his eyes, and often drinks by himself.

A joyless gloom pervades the atmosphere of the saloon that he frequents. He usually takes his beverage straight, and he is quite partial to cheese. He never mixes his drinks. The barkeeper does not need to ask him what he will take, for he always drinks out of the same bottle, and sighs as he wipes his chin on his sleeve and puts a piece of fly-blown lemon peel in his mouth. His cheerless, lugubrious countenance would look out of place anywhere except in the cave

of Trophonius or in a Greenback camp the day after
180 the election.

The more he drinks the more dejected he becomes. If
you meet him when he has taken, say, his fifth glass,
he will take you by the hand, and in a voice husky with
emotion, and old hand-made sour mash, he will tell you
that he is sorry that you should see him in this condition; he intimates that he always considered you the
best friend he had, and that he knows that he is doing
wrong in acting as he does. Then he weeps. When, with
the hope of making him take a more cheerful view of
things, you suggest that he take something with you,
he shakes his head in a despondent way and mutters
something about wishing he was dead, but he reaches
out for the bottle and takes a drink all the same. He
dries his eyes and tells you of his poor wife who died
several years ago, what a good woman she was, how
happy they were together (they use to lead a cat and
dog life, the neighbors say), and what a poor, lonely
wretch he has been since she was taken from him. At
this point he would give vent to his feelings in sobs
and tears, if his hiccough and the cheese on the lunch
counter did not engage his attention. The weeping
drunk man is a bilious and dyspeptic nuisance. There is
no pleasant feature about him.

When he is sober he may be a very pleasant acquaintance, but under the influence of stimulants he
becomes a solemn and dejected ass, whining about the
good times that have been, complaining and grieving
about the present and prophesying dire calamity in
the future. You may do all you can to cheer him up,
but it does no good; when you are gone he will stag-
ger around into the alley and sit down on a barrel
and weep until he feels that it is time to take another
drink.

MULCAHY'S COW

Boycotting still prevails in Ireland, and abounds in humorous incidents. Not long since, **Mr. Mulcahy**, who lives in a troubled district, and who is an enthusiastic land leaguer himself, had an unpleasant experience. The outlines of the story, which is a true one, and too good to be lost, are published in an English paper.

Mr. Mulcahy owned a valuable cow, to which he was very much attached, as he derived considerable profit from the sale of her milk. Unfortunately the animal became bilious, or afflicted with some other internal disorder, and Mulcahy was very much distressed in mind, body and estate, for the cow refused to let down the lacteal fluid with her accustomed regularity, and there was no telling how long the deadlock was go-

ing to last. Mulcahy was reliably informed that all
182 she needed to bring her to a healthy condition once
more was a pint of castor oil administered as a tonic.
The only hitch in the proceedings was caused by the
fact that all the castor oil in the neighborhood was
in possession of one Smith, a druggist, who, having
given offence to the land league, had been boycotted,
consequently Mulcahy and his cow were cut off from
their regular rations of castor oil. Mulcahy loved old
Ireland dearly, and was ready to be offered up on the
altar of his country several times a day, but what did
all that amount to compared with the milk his cow
refused to contribute to the sacred cause?

He finally came to the conclusion to go by night, like
Nicodemus, to the boycotted drug store without consulting with the land league. The night was dark and
dreary. Mulcahy reached the drug store unperceived.
The boycotted druggist was glad to see the only customer who had patronized him for weeks, and poured
out his thanks and the castor oil, and, with the latter
in a pint bottle, Mulcahy, the traitor to Ireland, slipped
out by the back gate and made for home.

As luck would have it, who should be coming up the
road but Messrs. O'Rourk, Donovan, Murphy, Mulli-
gan, O'Rafferty, O'Neil, O'Malley, Duffy and a lot more
of the boys, most of them with an "O" in front of their
names big enough to drive a cart through, and each
with a shillalah in each hand. They had no idea that
treason lurked in their midst. Mulcahy had, however,
taken a glass of the "crayture" with the boycotted
druggist, and when his friends smelled his breath
they were so carried away with enthusiasm for the
independence of their country that they took improp-
er liberties with his person in their wild search for the
bottle. When they found it their joy knew no bounds,

and without comparing it with Mulcahy's breath to
see if it agreed with the sample, they proceeded to *183*
appropriate the contents, the campaign plan being
that O'Rafferty, who had discovered it, should make
the opening speech. As for Mulcahy, he was sicker
than ever his cow dared be.

"Here," said O'Rafferty, raising aloft the bottle,
"here is health and prosperity to the Oirish republic
and bad luck to her inimies!"

As he was thirsty, and the rest of the patriots were
waiting impatiently for their turn, he put the bottle
to his mouth, intending to get all that was coming to
him, if not more—and he got it.

"I'm pizened! It's casthor oil!" he spluttered. The
others smelled the bottle, and knew at once that it
was not the bottle that flavored Mulcahy's breath.
They remembered Mulcahy's cow, and that nobody
but the boycotted druggist had castor oil. There was
circumstantial evidence enough to satisfy them that
Mulcahy had violated his oath, and had been trading
with a boycotted man. Usually, this means death. All
levity ceased. Mulcahy was sternly asked to explain
why he had violated his oath. He pleaded his case ably.
In the most pathetic language he portrayed the fate
of his family if he should lose his cow. He indignantly
denied that he was a traitor to Ireland. He was ready
to meet death on the scaffold, or on the field of battle
in defense of his country.

His judges were inexorable. He had violated his
oath, and must take the consequences. He was given
time to pray, which he did with a fervency that would
have melted a heart of stone. As soon as he said he
was ready, he was seized—and the pint of castor oil
poured down his throat, excepting, of course, as much
as O'Rafferty had already got away with. Mulcahy

184 was then set at liberty, but he was not in a condition to enjoy it very much. If he has occasion to go to that drug store again, he will probably select some other kind of tonic than castor oil.

WRITING UNDER DIFFICULTIES

Certain matters referred to in an editorial, headed "Some Editorial Duties," that we have just read, suggest that we outline to our readers the circumstances under which we usually write our articles. The following will give some idea of how we strive to do our duty, and what difficulties we have to contend with from day to day:

When we come down to the office in the morning we find several printers, hungry for copy. We ask them to please entertain themselves for a few moments by correcting proof, and promise them copy directly. Then we get a pencil and paper and begin dashing off—in search of a subject. Did the gentle reader ever try to capture a subject to write on, or try to write on it after he had caught it, while half a dozen printers in the next room were cussing him and threatening to strike if he didn't hand in some copy? If he didn't he has missed one of the most world-without-end-everlastingly exasperating jobs ever poor frail, finite man was called on to tackle.

We select a subject and have just begun to write an editorial entitled "An Analysis of the Sophistry of the Nothingness of Life," when we are interrupted by the entrance of a person who wants to know if we were striking at him in that article in our last issue in which we condemned the inhuman conduct of "a certain man in the Fifth ward." We try to pass it off as a joke by asking him what inhuman conduct he has *185* been guilty of, but this only exasperates him, and in self-defense we are forced to intimidate him. We proceed to do this with the only deadly weapon we ever carry—one of those long, heavy editorials cut from the Dallas *Herald*, with which we beat him over the head until he becomes insensible. Then the office boy, whose duty it is to attend to such details of business, drags him out.

This warms us up and leaves us in a splendid condition for writing mirthful paragraphs and facetious editorials, so we are about to start again on our Analysis article when a man comes in to ask if we exchange with the Nebraska *Nemesis*, published in the town where he formerly resided, and if we could give him the copy of the week before last. The *Nemesis* is one of our most valuable exchanges, because there is nothing in it worth clipping, and it therefore brings a good price as wrapping paper, but we lie about it—on principle—and tell him that we never heard of the *Nemesis*. As he leaves the office he collides with the man who brings in a new and original joke that he says never appeared in print before—in fact, the incident happened under his own observation only a few weeks ago. He suggests that we "just fix it up a little, you know," and it will be a good thing to put in the paper. As he begins to tell the entirely original joke, we recognize in it the emaciated remains of what was a robust and jovial young joke when it was brought to this country by the Puritan Fathers in the Mayflower. It shows traces of having traveled much since, although it has been half soled, patched in several places, and otherwise repaired. We get rid of him by referring him to the Commissioner of History

186 and Statistics, who is making a collection of all such relics of the old red sandstone period.

Then we take the scissors and slash out the first few items we find in the nearest exchange to our hand—County Treasurer Absconded—Another Stage Robbery—Gould has Purchased Two more Railroads—Oscar Wilde's Legs—that will choke off the printers till we get a start on our Analysis of the Sophistry, etc. But before we have got two lines written we find it is lunch time. During the remainder of the evening we succeed in writing two more lines, in intervals between the visits of our friends. First comes the old veteran, who used to be on intimate terms with Sam Houston, and who slaughtered Mexicans all through the fall of '35 and spring of '36, and failed to die when he should have died at San Jacinto, and who wishes to publish some reminiscences of the old days of the early settlements in Texas; then the man who has some business that calls him to Chicago, and who would be willing to furnish us with descriptive letters during his trip, if we would furnish him passes over the railroads. After him, the imbecile who suggests that we give the P. O. Dept. "a rasping," (he calls it) because the mails do not arrive on time. Next the drummer who says he has really no business with us, but "merely called in to see the two damned fools who write all that stuff in *Siftings*."

When we get through with all these it is time to go home, so the gentle reader will readily see that our time, during the day, is pretty well taken up, and so it goes on from day to day. We do all our editorial work at night, while the baby in the next room is howling under the influence of the colic.

THE TEXAS CLIMATE

The climate of Texas is an unabridged one, and we would be doing it an injustice if we did not devote some space to it in this paper.

When the pious old Spanish missionaries first came to Western Texas to convert the Indians, and everything else they could lay their hands on, to their own use, they noticed the extreme balminess of the atmosphere, the gorgeous Italian sunsets, and the superior quality of the climate. They were surprised that the Creator would waste so much good climate on the wicked heathen. Back where they came from, where all the folks were good Catholics and observed 211 holy days in the year, they couldn't raise as much climate per annum as they could harvest in Western Texas in one short week.

In the early days of the Republic of Texas, and even after annexation, many of the white men who came to Western Texas from all parts of the United States had strong sanitary reasons for preferring a change of climate. To be more explicit, the most of the invalids had been threatened with throat disease. So sudden and dangerous is this disease that the slightest delay in moving to a new and milder climate is apt to be fatal, the sufferer dying of dislocation of the spinal vertebra at the end of a few minutes and a rope. A great many men, as soon as they heard of Western Texas, left their homes in Arkansas, Indiana, and other States—left immediately, between two days—the necessity for their departure being so urgent that they were obliged to borrow the horses they rode to Texas on. All of these invalids recovered on reaching

Austin. In fact, they began to feel better, and consid-
188 ered themselves out of danger as soon as they crossed
the Brazos River. Some of those who would not have
lived twenty-four hours longer if they had not left
their old homes reached a green old age in Western
Texas, and, by carefully avoiding the causes that led
to their former troubles, were never again in any
danger of the bronchial affection already referred
to. As soon as it was discovered that the climate of
Western Texas was favorably disposed towards invalids, a large number of that class of unfortunates
came to Austin. Many well authenticated cases of re-
coveries are recorded. Men have been known to come
to Austin far gone in consumption, and so far recover
as to be able to run for office within a year, and to
be defeated by a large and respectable majority, all
owing to the atmosphere and the popularity of the
other candidate.

There is very little winter in Western Texas. But
for the northers Austin would have almost a tropical climate, as it is situated on the same parallel of
latitude as Cairo, in Egypt, where they have trop-
ics all the year around. As it is, there is seldom any
frost, although it is not an unusual thing for lumps of
ice several inches thick to be found—in tumblers, by
those who go to market in the early morning. Occasionally New Year's calls are made in white linen suits
and an intoxicated condition. Spring begins seriously
in February. The forest trees put on their beautiful
garments of green, and the fruit trees come out in
bloom. Prairie flowers and freckles come out in this
month, and the rural editor begins to file away spring
poetry. In February stove pipes are laid away in the
wood-shed, and the syrup of squills and kough kure
man puts a coat of illuminated texts on the garden

fence. Seedticks are not pulled until April, but after the middle of March there is no danger of the mos-   quito crop being frozen. Early in March the doctors oil their stomach pumps, for the green mulberry ripens about that time, and has to be removed from the schoolboy.

Toward the middle of April the early peach appears, and all nature—and the druggist—smiles, ushering in the long and lingering summer time when the ice cream festivals of the church of the Holy Embarrassment rageth from one end of fair and sunny Texas to the other. Such is a short synopsis of the varying features of the Texas climate.

WORK

Work is what men are paid for doing. Some kinds of work are paid for by the yard, some by the day and some by the job. Railroad contractors, for instance, are paid by the yard, street car drivers by the day, and portrait painters by the job. Legislators are paid both by the day and by the job. When a certain thing is done—an act performed for money—it is called work. When the same thing is done merely to pass time it is called pleasure. A man will go prowling around all day through marshes and bogs in search of snipe; and come home at night, worn and tired, with eight or ten poor little birds, the market price of which is about 25 cents for the lot, and he will say that he had a glorious day's sport. That is pleasure. If that same man was paid good wages to pursue and harass snipe every day in the year it would be work, and he would think this a weary world, and wish he were dead.

Some people get an immense amount of so-called
pleasure out of the flowing bowl. But take one of
these people and pay him fifteen dollars a week to
disorganize his internal machinery with adulterated
alcohol and drugged malt liquors; have it in the contract that he must take enough to make him sick at
the stomach once every twenty-four hours, and make
him sleep on hard benches and attend to his duties
till 11 or 12 o'clock every night. He will call that work
and won't like it, while under the name of pleasure he
would gladly give it his undivided attention 365 days
in the year.

What we are compelled to do we call work, and
mostly every one of us thinks that the work he has
to do is more severe than what those in other voca-
tions have to perform. The horny-handed farmer, as
he earns his bread by the sweat of his brow and the
jolts he gets as he plows through roots and snags, believes his the hardest work of all, and when he thinks
of the editor sitting in his easy-chair, dashing off eloquent and humorous editorials in his leisure moments,
he gnashes his teeth and swears if the idea is suggested to him that an editor ever knows anything
of work. And the editor, as he toils over an idea that
he cannot find words to express, while the printer,
in the most aggravating manner, stands around on
one leg impatiently waiting for copy, and muttering
something about not getting to press in time for the
next mail—that editor, as he scratches his head in a
vain endeavor to remember whether one "r" is all that
belongs to the word harass, wishes that he was only
a farmer—one of those simpleminded grangers who
need never be in a hurry to get to the end of a row,
who is never too busy to sit on the fence and discuss
politics, and whose severest labor is in suppressing his

190

robust appetite with fresh-laid eggs and curds and cream. So it is in every department of life; we have *191* all got work to do, and each of us is inclined to think his lot the hardest. But the cultivation of a cheerful and hopeful spirit and the occasional reflection that if it were twice as bad with us it would be worse, will do much toward making us contented and better prepared to wrestle with the labors, cares and duties that the injudicious act of that old ancestor of ours left us as an heritage.

ROUGH ON WORMS

Old Uncle Mose went into Levi Schaumburg's store, on Austin avenue, to buy a silk handkerchief, but was almost paralyzed on learning the price. Levi explained that the high price of silk goods was caused by some disease among the silk worms.

"How much does yer ask for dis heah piece ob tape?" asked the old man.

"Ten cents," was the reply

"Ten cents? Jewhilikins! So de tape has riz, too. I s'pose de cause ob dat am because dar's somefin' de matter wid de tape-wums. Dis gwine ter be a mighty tough yeah on wums, anyhow."

PETER B. LEE

One day last week, we received a complimentary call from Mr. Peter B. Lee. He was not owing us a call, but he dropped in all the same, as he was passing through the capital en route for San Antonio, where there was a great demand for him, so he said.

There are very few editors, or printers, who require any information about Peter B. Lee. He is a nomadic printer who is always on the tramp. That's the type of a man he is. In his official capacity, as a tramp, he has visited almost every town and city in the United States and the Territories, besides a large portion of the two Canadas. He never stops in a town longer than a few days, unless he becomes too much tangled 193 up in the streets to find his way out. As soon as he has accumulated, by setting type, a cash balance of a dollar and a half, he invests it at the nearest saloon, and then meanders off in a hesitating, uncertain kind of a way, in the direction of the next town. He never forgets himself so far as to become beastly drunk, neither does he ever lay himself open to the suspicion of being entirely sober. He is an original character.

In traveling he disdains to ride on railroads, possibly because the money he would squander on the conductor can be more advantageously invested in his favorite beverage. His baggage consists of a bundle of newspapers, donated by the last newspaper office he visited. Mr. Lee does not carry these newspapers in order to improve his mind by reading, while resting from his pedestrian exercises. He swaps them off for "grub," as he calls it. The farmer who is craving for intellectual food, in the shape of a late newspaper, willingly fills up the empty pedestrian with corn bread and buttermilk for a late copy of the N. Y. *Herald*.

As we have already stated, he called on us. After entertaining the printers for a short time, and asking how far it was to El Paso, and if there was a good show for buttermilk along the route, he approached the editorial throne, and asked if we had any objection to his encumbering himself with a few of our exchanges. We had no objection. He went to the table where the exchanges are kept, or rather where they are not kept, so many of them falling prey to the exchange fiend, and began to pick out those that were best calculated to instruct and elevate the farmer. As he pawed over the papers, Mr. Lee indulged in a very

interesting and confidential conversation with him-
194 self, utterly unconscious that he was saying as witty
things as we ever heard. He took up a copy of the
Houston *Post*, and holding it out at arm's length, said,
"Ah! that's a very good paper to put a man to sleep.
I'll get a night's lodging for that. That paper will furnish two men with all the sleep they want. I'll get
a good bed and sleep all night, and the farmer will
try to read, and he will sleep all the next day. Do you
know, Mr. Editor, that I inadvertently was the cause
of the death of a worthy man, near Fort Worth, last
summer?"

"Did you talk him to death?"

"No, sir; I did not. I gave him a copy of the Houston
Post and one of the Dallas *Herald* for my dinner. He
rashly undertook to read them both. He fell asleep,
and although every effort was made by the ablest
physicians for three whole days, he never could shake
off the drowsiness; so they buried him in a shady dell,
where the flowerets droop. No—no, I didn't talk him
to death. I've got no flow of language at all, except
when I am perfectly sober, so there is no danger of
my talking anybody into the silent tomb."

And just here Mr. Lee kept on picking out the papers
he wanted, commenting on their mechanical appearance, financial standing, or making confidential
remarks aloud to himself about the personal appearance and habits of the editors, with whom he seemed
to be personally intimate. He spoke in high terms of
the fine typographical appearance of the Houston
Age, and intimated that he and the editor, whom he
called Dan, were bosom friends; that they had often
helped each other to pass the flowing bowl, etc., etc.
Mr. Lee complimented the size and make-up of the San
Antonio *Express*, for which he claimed some credit

to himself, as he had given some practical hints and suggestions to Mr. Grice, the editor, who was also an intimate friend, and to whom his, Lee's, purse was always open. Mr. Lee used some very expressive language in reference to the local editor of the *Express*, who had intimated that he was given to too much wine, and irregular habits.

"And here is the Washington *Critic*," remarked our visitor; "it is an admirably edited paper of the Star Route persuasion. If I can't get a 'hand-out' for it, I can at least expatiate on its merits from a journalistic standpoint. And here is the Austin *Wochenblatt*. I will take that along, and tender it to some hardy German settler just about dinner time. An occasional plate of *saur kraut* is said to produce a beneficial effect on the kidneys." So saying, he folded up his exchanges, and after asking permission to use some twine from a ball, he started for the door. Just as he reached it a sudden thought struck him. Coming back, he said, "I wish to call your attention to an extraordinary circumstance."

"What is it?"

"That I didn't take the ball of twine when I had such a good chance!" And once more pressing our editorial hand, he wafted himself out of the door in the direction of El Paso, leaving nothing behind to remind us of his visit, except a well-defined smell of an inferior article of Austin whiskey.

THE COLORED COOK

There is quite a variety of colored cooks infesting the kitchens of the Southern end of the United States of North America at the present day. They vary in color from the somber shades of a burned stump in a dark alley, at midnight, to the mellow tints of a ripe pumpkin tinged with the rays of the rising sun. They vary in other respects. The young one is more impudent and less respectful than the old one. When she comes in search of a "place," she is apt to say that a "culled wash lady" told her that the "white woman what lived here wanted to hire a cook." But they all resemble each other in one particular—their ignorance of cookery is 20° above proof, and their unconsciousness of their ignorance may safely be said to register at least 145° Fahrenheit in the shade.

We have not space to describe all the varieties of the colored cook, but will tell what we know of the commonest type, that represented by our artist at the head of this article—the culinary artist, who is fat, black, and forty years of age or thereabout. She is proud of having "b'longed to de ole jedge 'fo' de wah," and she is fond of comparing the present with the past. Her comparisons are not complimentary to the present, for her surroundings are, to her, as the gloomy ruins of social and material things standing out against a brilliant and golden tinted background "ob de gorjusness ob de good ole days."

With the loyalty of her race, she is faithful to her old master and mistress to the extent of calling on them for the loan of half a dollar whenever she is financially embarrassed.

She seldom stays at any one place more than three months at a time. When hired, she promises to come on Thursday—the day the old cook intends leaving—but she does not come until the following Monday evening, when she arrives accompanied by a small trunk with wallpaper pasted over the outside of it, and a large bundle of her "things" tied up in a patch-work bedspread. During the first few days she acts so that her mistress absorbs the idea that the new cook is a treasure. But her satisfaction in, and her admiration of, her treasure receives successive and severe shocks as the idiosyncrasies of the cook's character begin to develop.

She can cook a chicken, but all the colored people can do that. It is a talent that is hereditary. Beyond that her capacity is limited. She breathes on the plates and polishes them on her sleeve before putting them on the table. She develops religious proclivities which necessitate her attendance at church three times on Sunday, at prayer meeting on Wednesday, and choir

practice on Saturday night. She is also a member of
198 the "Benevolent Order of the Sisters of the Mysterious Ten Wise Virgins," the weekly meetings of which require her attention on Tuesday night. Thus her mistress has only three evenings in the week on which she feels at liberty to entertain her friends at her own house.

The favorite dissipation of the colored cook, besides religious observances, consists in sitting down on the kitchen doorstep to rest, and going to sleep there while the biscuits burn to a cinder, and the coffee boils over and mixes with the cabbage and other fruits in the adjacent skillet. She has days on which she suffers with "a misery" in her head, probably from too much religious observance on the previous evening, and on these days she takes a gloomy view of life, breaks dishes, forgets to put baking powder in the batter cakes, and manufactures coffee of the kind that leaves successive circles of an alluvial deposit on the inside of the cup. It is not well to remonstrate with her on these occasions. If you do she will talk to herself confidentially in a low tone of voice during the next two days about being overworked. In the cotton picking season nothing short of lessons on the piano, the use of the parlor to receive her company in, and seven nights out in the week, will induce the average colored cook to remain at her post of duty and continue the destruction of expensive groceries. Cotton picking, with banjo accompaniments, and the dance at night in the barn, have attractions that no pecuniary offer will outweigh, and the cotton field is to the cook what the fashionable watering place is to her young mistress.

When she comes to hire she tells her employer that she is not married. After awhile, when the latter notices the frequent appearance of "a cullud ge'mman" about the kitchen and the cook's boudoir, and brings *199* her to task for having concealed the fact that she was married, she replies, "Fo' de Lawd! We isn't married; we jes took up wid one anodder."

Honesty is her strong point; she can be trusted with a dollar to take to market in the morning, and she will invest fifty cents of it in provisions and cheerfully turn over fifteen cents of change to her employer on her return. The appetite of the colored cook is something that the columns of this paper are too limited in extent to describe.

ST. PATRICK'S DAY

Saint Patrick is a saint about whom very little is known, and that little is very uncertain. He was born of English parents in France, on the 4th of July, A.D. 400, which may account, in some measure, for his having been one of the first men of that century. A few years afterwards, on New Year's day, A. D. 403, he was born in Scotland of unknown parentage. A year or so later, he saw the light for the first time on the anniversary of the battle of New Orleans in Holland; that is, St. Patrick was born in Holland. The anniversary of the battle of New Orleans was not born in Holland. Whenever, in the goodness of your heart, you undertake to give St. P. a write up, you are sure to get things mixed. The number of St. Patrick's mothers is also involved in uncertainty, but there must have been half a dozen of them, at least, and they were, doubtless, are very proud of him, each one claiming he got his good looks from herself. St. Pat-

200 rick's father is also involved in more or less obscurity, but there is reason to believe that his maiden name, before he was made a saint, was O'Rafferty. The only absolutely sure thing about S!. Patrick is, that he was not born here in Austin, Teyas.

Very little is positively known about St. Patrick's boyhood, except that it is probable he had one or two boyhoods. He seems to have had everything in duplicate and triplicate. The ancient archives of Paris show that a boy answering the description of St. Patrick was arrested for disturbing people with a nigger-shooter in A. D. 415.

Historians are a unit that he dislocated his ankle by being bounced from the rear of a bobtail car, in New York, as early as A. D. 410. There is documentary evidence to show that St. Patrick manifested signs of piety at a very early age, as he was given to crawling under circus tents, tying tin cans to dogs' tails, and to staying out late at night, being somewhat of a convivial turn of mind, as are his spiritual descendants to this day.

There can be no doubt but that he landed in Ireland for the first time in the spring of A. D. 432, on the east coast of the island. As a matter of history, he also landed for the first time a few years later on the west coast, and for about forty years he kept on landing for the first time, and at different places. Almost everything else about St. Patrick, except the facts already given, is somewhat obscure.

He found Ireland inhabited by savage tribes, some of whom had come over from New York, and he converted them. They became good Christians, and St. Patrick never had to call on them twice for their pew rent. St. Patrick also found the island infested with copperheads and other snakes of the dangerous kind.

He converted them, too. We do not know into what he converted them, but we have a theory that he *201* converted them into that class of land leaguers who shoot poor people for honestly paying their rent, who mutilate cows, and batter flocks of sheep to death. What goes to strengthen this theory is the fact that there are no *bona fide* snakes or reptiles in Ireland.

St. Patrick is supposed to have died in A. D. **493**, but where, nobody knows. It is also very certain that nobody knows what he died of, or what doctor was called in. As he was nearly one hundred years old when he died, it could not have been teething nor cholera infantum that carried him off. As far as we know, St. Patrick did not belong to any fire company. He is buried all over Europe. We have never heard of his having left a widow, but as there are vast numbers of Sons of St. Patrick, we infer that he was married frequently; and that one of his wives must have been a widow with twenty or thirty children. St. Patrick left no property. *Requiescat in pace.*

FUTURE SCULPTOR
−OR CONGRESSMAN

"What are you going to make out of your boy Bill?" asked one Austin parent of another.

"I think Bill will be a great sculptor," was the reply

"Has he any talent that way?"

"I should say so. He chisels all the other boys out of their marbles."

THE
CONFIDENTIAL
DRUNK

The man who gets confidential when he becomes drunk, is one of the most tiresome of
the different varieties of men who look upon
the rye when it is flavored with lemon peel. He may
be a very taciturn man in his total abstinence moods,
but when he gets under the influence of a succession
of cocktails he tries to tell all he knows, and his bursts
of confidence are really painful to his friends and ac-
quaintances. He not only tells all that he knows, but
much that he does not know familiarly enough to talk
about with certainty. When in an inebriated condition,
he will stretch his imagination until you can hear it
crack and ravel at the edges, and he will tell massive
and voluminous lies about the extent of his business,
the colossal influence he has in politics, his intimacy
with great men, and such matters. It is not what he

says, but the manner in which he says it, that makes his outbursts of confidential mendacity exasperating. *203* He makes a great show of taking you to one side and unwinding ponderous falsehoods, intended, as he says, especially for our own ear. He puts his hand on your shoulder and whispers down the back of your neck, while you can smell his hilarious breath as it tickles the bare place just back of your ear. Then, forgetting that the matter has been communicated to you confidentially, he will tell the same thing, in a loud tone of voice, to the barkeeper. He breaks out in winks and nods, and dark hints and mysterious allusions regarding something that (owing to private information he has received, and which he is not at liberty to divulge), he is satisfied will be made public and astonish the community in a few days. He gradually becomes incoherent and mixes up an account of one of his youthful adventures with something he read in the last number of the New York *Weekly*. It is a good time to leave him then, and if he cannot secure another victim he will sit down in a chair and talk to himself until he goes to sleep. The person who drinks with the rest of the party will not notice the peculiar atrocities and idiotic proceedings of the confidential or any other bacchanalian reveler. The foolishness and absurdity of their actions are only perceptible to the man who does not drink strong liquors, "one of whom we are which."

ROUGH TRANSLATION

A young lady moving in the most exalted social circles of Austin, after much toil and practice at the piano, learned to play with considerable dexterity a piece entitled "Picnic Polka." It is something after the style of the celebrated "Battle of Prague." The lis-

tener can readily distinguish the roar of the artillery
204 the rattle of the musketry, the shouts of the soldiers
and the groans of the dying. In the "Picnic Polka"
the noise of the wind among the trees and the joyous
carols of the birds are reproduced, the finale being a
thundershower which disturbs the sylvan revelers.

It happens that a country cousin is in town just
now, and the young lady thought she would play the
piece to him and hear his comment. He is a plain, sim-
ple-minded youth, and although not very bright, is
very appreciative. She told him what the piece was
and then proceeded to give him the "Picnic Polka."
The first notes are rather slow and hesitating, the
idea sought to be conveyed being the solemn solitude
of the forest, through which the gentle zephyr (not
heifer) sighs. After she got through with this preface,
she asked him if he did not almost imagine himself in
a lodge in some vast wilderness. He replied that he
thought all that slowness meant the delay in getting
off. Said he, "There is always some plaguey cuss who
oversleeps himself and keeps everybody else waiting."

She did not care to discuss the point with the ignorant fellow, so, to conceal her emotions, she once more
let herself out on the piano. The woods were filled
with music. The mockingbird whistled as if his throat
would split, the cuckoo filled the sylvan bowers with
his repeated cry, while ever and anon the mournful
cooing of the dove interrupted the mating song of
the lark.

"There, now, I guess you know what that sounds
like?" she said, as she paused.

"You mean that 'tootle, tootle, tootle, chug, chug,
chug?' You just bet I understand that. Many is the
time at a picnic I've heard it from the mouth of a
demijohn, or the bunghole of a beer-keg."

Her first impulse was to hurl the piano stool at him, but it passed off, and once more she went at the piano *205* as if it was the young man's head and was insured for double its value. The thunder growled, the lightning flashed (from her eyes) and the first heavy drops are heard upon the leaves. She banged and mauled the keys at a fearful rate; peal after peal of deafening thunder perturbed the atmosphere and re-echoed in still louder reverberation until it wound up in one appalling clap as a grand finale. Then, turning to the awe-struck youth, she said: "I suppose you have heard something like that before?"

"Yes; that's what the fellow with linen pants said when he sat down on the custard pie."

The audience found himself alone, but he picked up his hat and sauntered out into the street, densely unconscious that he had said anything out of the way.

SIFTINGS

YES SIREE BOB

Col. Pompernickel, one of the leading German manufacturers of New Braunfels, Texas, who was in Austin not long since, tells a story upon himself when, as a raw lad, he was making his first efforts to master the difficulties of the English language. All foreigners agree that the English is the hardest of all languages to acquire; so does the Colonel.

He had already learned the force and signification of "sir," and very naturally concluded that siree was its feminine. Being seated at a table opposite a very polite lady, who asked him if he would partake of a certain dish, he replied, "Yes siree."

The laughter which followed somewhat disconcert-206 ed our hero, but he turned to a friend at his right and inquired what mistake he had made. His friend informed him that he should have said, "Yes siree bob." The roar of laughter from the audience, who now began to take an interest in the young German, confused him very much. In the midst of the confusion his left-hand neighbor kindly whispered something in his ear which encouraged him so much that he braced himself for a third effort. Once more the lady inquired: "Will you have a biscuit, sir?" when he answered: "Yes siree bobtail."

IT WAS NOT IN HIS HEAD

Uncle Mose went into an Austin Avenue drug store, yesterday, and asked, "What has yer dat's good for a headache?"

The druggist took down a large bottle of salts of ammonia, or some such stuff, and told Uncle Mose to smell. As it was a free thing, he drew in a healthy inspiration, that took away his breath. It was ten minutes before he could talk, and when he did say something it was that he would "bust" the druggist's head wide open if he came at him with that bottle again.

"But how about the headache?" asked the druggist.

"How de debbel can I tell ontil I goes home and asks de ole 'ooman. Sh'e de one what's got de misery in de head."

NEW BRAND OF SMOKING TOBACCO

A rough-looking customer from Onion Creek, came into a tobacco store on Austin Avenue, and said he wanted some smoking tobacco.

"What brand do you prefer?" asked the tobacconist.

"I want a package of Emergency."

"Emergency? I never heard of any such tobacco."

"All I know," said the man from the country, is that Uncle Bill had the toothache last night, and smoked all night, and I asked him which was the best kind of tobacco; and he said no tobacco was equal to the Emergency. So I thought if none of 'em was equal to Emergency, that must be the best the market affords. If you haven't got the Emergency, I reckon I'll have to try some other store."

A CALCULATION

An old darkey who works around town by the day, and who is very proud of his reputation for extraordinary ability in ciphering, called on Gilhooly yesterday with a view to get a settlement, in cash, for work done in Gilhooly's garden.

"Well, Uncle Ben," said the Major. "How much do I owe you?"

"Ise worked fur ye 'leben days at a dollar a day, boss, an' if yer hand me a piece' of paper an' a pencil, I'll cipher it out fur yer."

Uncle Ben got the paper, and pretending to figure on it, he said, " 'Leben days at a dollar a day. Lemme see, ought's a ought, cipher's a cipher, figure's a figure, two ter carry, an' one ter throw away. 'Leben dollars, by gosh! Boss, yer owes me prezactly 'leben dollars."

A HEROIC ACT

In no city in the United States was there more intense indignation at the shooting of President Garfield than in Austin. There was quite a crowd of the leading and most influential citizens discussing the

tragedy, when a big bully spoke up, and said, "For my
208 part, I am glad Garfield was shot. He ought to have
been shot long ago."

A small, one-armed, poorly dressed man reached out
and knocked the bully down. Both parties were strangers. There was a roar of applause, as the bully picked
himself up and slunk off. The crowd gathered around
the one-armed man, who was the hero of the hour.
Prominent Democrats pressed his hand, and expressed
their admiration of his heroism. He took it very mod-
estly, merely saying that he, and his father before him,
were Jeffersonian Democrats; that none of the family
had ever voted the Republican ticket; that he was poor,
having lost all his property, including negroes, and his
arm, during the war, and was in feeble health besides,
yet he would knock down any man who expressed satisfaction at the shooting of the President.

There were murmurs of approval. A hurried con-
sultation. The one-armed Confederate was invited up
to the bar, and fifteen dollars, that had been hastily
collected, was presented to him. He refused to take it.
He was insulted, but was finally induced to accept it
as a temporary loan.

Later in the afternoon one of the gentlemen who
had witnessed the scene in the saloon, met the one-
armed man, who was slightly inebriated, and said,
"You did just right to knock that scoundrel down. He
deserved all he got."

"He thought he deserved more," responded the one-
armed man; "he got half the money, and wanted more
because I hit him on the nose; but he don't deserve
any more, for I had to do all the talkin'."

The Austin man, who had contributed liberally,
gasped for air, while the ex-Confederate drifted down
Austin Avenue in the direction of the nearest saloon.

TOO MUCH PROVERB

While the prisoners in the Austin jail were out in the yard a few days ago, two of them who were under sentence to the Penitentiary, were heard comparing notes about as follows, "I don't believe in proverbs," said prisoner No. 1; "it is believing in proverbs that brings me here."

"How so?" said No. 2.

"Well, you see when I was a boy, I often seen folks pick up pins, and when I asked them why they did it, they said

'If you see a pin and let it lay,
You will have bad luck all the day.' "

"Yes, that's so. I've heard that myself."

"Well, it don't work. I have picked up a pin, and I have had bad luck ever since. I was arrested the very same day, and now I've got to go to the Penitentiary for three years."

"What has that to do with picking up pins?" asked No. 2.

"Well, you see the pin I picked up was a diamond pin worth $150. I believed in the proverb about having good luck, so I picked up the pin in a showcase, but they telephoned for the police and here I am," and he winked at the jailer.

The other prisoner thought for a moment, and then he said, "When I come to think of it, proverbs are what have brought me to this fix."

"How so?" asked the man who had picked up the pin for good luck.

"Well, I had heard about horseshoes bringing good luck, so I picked up horseshoes. Horseshoes were my weakness."

"Them horseshoes you went off with were fastened
210 on to another fellow's horse, weren't they?" queried
No. 1.

"Jess so. When I get out I'm not going to tamper
with any more proverbs," remarked No. 2.

"Me, neither," responded No. 1.

"Fall in, boys," said the jailer, and they went back to
their cozy retreats on the inside of the jail.

HALAF OF A TOLLAR

Gilhooly went into Mose Schaumburg's
store, on Austin Avenue, to buy an umbrella. Mose showed him two kinds of
umbrellas, which looked very much alike,
one of which was a dollar and the other a
dollar and a half. Gilhooly examined them
critically, and asked, "What is the difference between them?"

"Halaf of a tollar," responded Mose.

A WIFE'S DEVOTION

About 3 o'clock yesterday afternoon a large crowd
of men and boys, near the corner of Main Street and
Austin Avenue, were treated to an exhibition of wife-
ly devotion, which could not but affect the strongest
heart. The woman had found her husband lying in a
beastly state of intoxication in an alley. Instead of
being exasperated, she gently turned him over to a
comfortable position, and, running her hand into his
vest pocket, she extracted a twenty dollar bill, and remarked, "I reckon I've got the dead wood on that new
bonnet I've been sufferin' for." She made a straight
streak for the nearest millinery shop. Strong men

wiped the moisture from their eyes at the wife's heroic devotion to a husband who had, by strong drink, *211* brought himself so low as to neglect to provide his wife with the common necessaries of life.

DIDN'T KNOW ANY NEWS— MAN SHOT NEAR AUSTIN

"You picked the pecans on Onion creek, you say?" said an Austin reporter yesterday to a young man on a wagon filled with pecans.

"Yes, sir," he replied, "that's where they came from."

"Many up there?"

"Plenty of them."

"Believe I'll try a few," quizzed the reporter, taking a big handful of the pecans.

"I'll sell you a whole peck for fifty cents," said the man, with swelling eyes.

"Only want a few. Say, do you know any news?"

"Not a bit, sir; everything is very dull up our way."

"Don't you know anything?"

"Well, I believe I did hear some news yesterday."

"What was it?" asked the reporter, cracking a pecan.

"There was a man got 18 buckshot in him near where I live?"

"Who shot him?"

"I did."

"What did you shoot him for?"

"For stealing some of my pecans out of my wagon," said the countryman, reaching for his shotgun.

The reporter hastily replaced the pecans in the wagon, and after calling the countryman "Colonel," disappeared around the corner. That evening he told his employers that they must insure his life for $50,000, or he would resign.

A ROUGH GUESS

A small boy darted into a drug store on Austin Avenue and said to the clerk, "Gimme some pizen to kill bed bugs."

"How much?" asked the man of drugs, thinking about the price.

"How much? Well, I reckon if they was all corralled they would fill a quart cup."

We regret to add that the boy came out of one of the finest residences in Austin.

TOO MUCH LEARNING

"What did you do with that letter that was on my table?" asked Gus De Smith, of the colored boy who cleans up his room.

"I tuk it to de post office, sah, and put it in de hole."

"What did you do that for? Did you not see that there was no address on the envelope?"

"I saw dar was no writin' on de 'velope, but I 'lowed ye did dat ar on purposs, so I couldn't tell who yer was a-writin' to. I's an edicated negro, I is."

BETTER LATE THAN NEVER

Two young men who move in the very best Austin society, went on a spree not long since. After they were pretty well under way one of them said, in an inebriated tone of voice, "Let's bid each other good-night, Bill."

"Why, you ain't going home already? It's right in the shank of the evening."

"Of coursh I'm not goin' home now, but after a while we won't know each ozzer from a shide of sole-leather, sho lets shay goodnight right now before it'sh too late." They embraced.

HARD TO TELL

"Have you read Governor Roberts' book?" asked Gilhooly of Gus De Smith.

"Yes," responded Gus; "there are eight of us young men at our boarding-house on Austin Avenue, and we have all read it carefully."

"What do you all think of it?"

"Well, you see, there are eight chapters in the book, and each one of us thinks that one chapter in particular should have been omitted."

"Which chapter?"

"That's what no two of us agreed on. Each one of us thought a different chapter was the worst."

CHOKING JUDAS ISCARIOT

Every year, at Christmas, the San Antonio Mexicans celebrate a kind of imitation of the "Passion Play," called "Pastores." The Virgin Mary, the apostles, including Judas Iscariot; all appear and act their parts. On the last occasion of this play, Judas was missing.

"What has become of Judas?" asked one of the spectators, of St. Peter, with whom he was well acquainted.

"Judas be damned!" was the reply; "last year we had to choke him to make him give back the thirty pieces of silver that we gave him in the play, so this year we apostles won't let him stick his nose inside of the circus tent."

REV. WHANGDOODLE BAXTER

The Rev. Whangdoodle Baxter, an Austin colored clergyman, wished to hint to Uncle Nace, who is his near neighbor, that a gift of a cord of firewood would be very gratefully accepted. Uncle Nace, by-the-way,

does not like Whangdoodle much. Finally, says Whang-
214 doodle, insinuatingly, "Uncle Nace, I's gwine ter be
powerful hard up for firewood dis winter. Can't yer
gimme a load?"

Uncle Nace looked all around as if he was afraid
of being overheard, and then he said, "Parson, is you
werry pertickler whar de wood comes from?"

Parson Whangdoodle supposed this to mean that
Uncle Nace was going to give him some stolen wood,
so he replied, "Uncle Nace, as long as I gets de wood,
I don't keer much whar it comes from."

"Den, Parson, you don't keer whose wood you bums
up."

"Hit's all de same ter me, Uncle Nace."

"Well, I am gwine," said Nace.

"Whar is yer gwine?"

"Ter lock up my wood-shed."

ON HIS FEET AGAIN

Col. Bill Snort, editor of the Crosby County *Clarion
and Farmers' Vindicator*, was in Austin a few days
ago, and paid a complimentary visit to *Texas Siftings*.

There was a merchant in his town who had written
us, offering to subscribe for our great weekly if we
would wait for the cash till fall, so we asked Snort
how the merchant was coming on, if he had recovered
from the effects of his failure a few months ago.

"Well, he is on his feet again."

"Glad to hear it. Is he making money?"

"Not much. When I said he was on his feet again, I
only meant he had to sell his horse and buggy, and do
all his riding on foot."

THE MODEST DRUMMER

Ike Schwindelmeyer is a relative of old man Schwindelmeyer, of the well-known Galveston firm of Schwindelmeyer & Co. Ike is a recent importation from Germany, and travels for the firm. He has a very great opinion of himself, and thinks that Schwindelmeyer & Co. own this world, and have a builders' lien on the next. Not long since young Ike Schwindelmeyer visited Austin. On the morning of his arrival, after breakfast, he started up the Avenue. It happened that the funeral procession of a prominent citizen was also proceeding up the Avenue. Ike was about abreast of the hearse, and the gentlemen on the sidewalks removed their hats, and remained uncovered until the hearse had passed. Ike took this all to himself, and politely returned the salutations with some pleasant remark, as "A peautiful morning, shentlemens!" or " how ish yerself today?"

There was a larger crowd of gentlemen at the corner of Pecan street, and when Ike and the hearse came up they all took off their hats reverently. Ike was moved at this universal homage, and exclaimed, half confidentially, to himself:

"I vonder who tole 'em I vash traveling for Schwindelmeyer & Co?"

ANSWERS TO CORRESPONDENTS

The editor who attends to this column solicits questions, because he is full of valuable information and statistics, and is surcharged with a load of household receipts that he wants to get rid of. When he is not tapped occasionally, and some of his information allowed to run out, he becomes absolutely dangerous on account of discharging loads of information at irregular and frequent intervals. No one in the office is safe from these missiles. No longer ago than yesterday he seriously injured the devil, who was foraging for copy, by the unexpected discharge of a chunk of "Religious statistics," and last week he threw up a "Solution of the Irish question" that came within an ace of leaving his partner a cripple for life. Last Friday night he gave birth to a double-leaded receipt for taking grease spots out of woolen goods, that shook the office from foundation to dome, bruised the mailing clerk's foot, and pied a patent medicine electrotype cut. Under these circumstances it is hoped that the public will see the necessity of sending on questions at once.

TEXAS SIFTINGS

FROM LAURA B. M., KAUFMAN, TEXAS:

I hear a great deal about a new fashionable folly the decoration of plates by amateur artists. How is the thing done, and can you describe what the decoration consists of?

We have had several plates decorated lately by female members of our family The way they did it was after this fashion: They first warmed the plate, then they laid on it several slices of the breast of a turkey a second joint, some cranberries, dressing (without onions), and a couple of boiled Irish potatoes. Try that sort of decoration, and your friends will appreciate your artistic ability.

FROM J. P. C., MILLICAN, TEXAS:

I want to learn to play on the flute. How would you advise me to go about it? Will I need a teacher?

No; you do not need a teacher, but you had better borrow a flute. It would be well at first to select some retired spot where you can practice undisturbed. We would suggest that you hire or buy a ship and go out on the wild, tempestuous ocean—the ever changing sea—out amid the weird winds' wild roar, and the bilious billows' moan. There, far out of sight of land, with naught to disturb you but the voice of the cheerful sea gull as he skims the ocean blue and chants his merry lay you can heave your to-gallan's'l, box your anchor, and toot and toot and flute till you can't rest. After you practice for a year or two amid those surroundings, we would advise that you go west and herd sheep or the balance of your days. If that does not effect a cure, your case is a hopeless one.

FROM B. McC. TOPEKA, KANSAS:

What do Chinamen use to give gloss to the shirts they wash?

We have taken pains to find out exactly what they do use. We interviewed a Chinaman, who, after some persuasion, divulged the secret, and we made him write it down for us so that there could be no mistake. You first wash the shirt and dry it, then you put some

市 迤 珠

on it. That's what he called it, but as we can't pronounce it without stuttering, we give it in his own handwriting. Then the shirt should be ironed. If these directions are carefully followed out, so the Chinaman assures us, you will make a success of the business.

FROM W. J. K., PALESTINE, TEXAS:

I am a young man of limited means; I have only been in the State a short time, and it doesn't suit me to stay here longer. Would you advise me to go to Mexico? Please advise me at length through the columns of your paper.

As you have not given us full particulars, we are hardly in a position to advise you understandingly. In a general way however, we would suggest that if you have stolen a horse, the safest thing you could do would be to get over into Mexico as quickly as possible, even

if you have to steal another horse to get there on; but if you have only killed an acquaintance, there is no reason why you should put yourself to the inconvenience of running off to Mexico. Stay where you are, prove insanity self-defense, or an alibi, and become a leading citizen.

FROM TOM B., MOBILE, ALABAMA:
Is the watermelon a fruit or a vegetable?

That depends upon how you acquire possession of the melon. If you buy it on the street, it is a mere vegetable, but if you have to crawl on your stomach about half a mile through high weeds on a moonlight night to steal it, while the old Granger who owns it is asleep, then it is a rich and luscious tropical fruit. Your question is unseasonable.

FROM J. P. C., ROCKDALE, TEXAS:
We want to procure an artesian well in our town. About how much does a good artesian well cost, and are all artesian wells alike?

All artesian wells are not alike. Ready-made wells, sold at country stores, are not to be recommended. They are liable to crack, fray at the edges, and bag at the knees. The cost of an Artesian well depends on its depth. You should hire men and bore your well right on the place where you want to use it. In that way you save freight, and give your townsmen the opportunity to joke about bores, and to turn loose on the workmen that old gag about getting a long well.

FROM J. A. P., TOPEKA, KANSAS:

220 I have been noticing a good many references in the papers to Oscar Wilde, but have as yet learned but little of him. Who and what is he? I would like you to answer if it does not take up too much of your valuable space.

FROM ROBERT J., BRENHAM, TEXAS:

The "disunwellness" that you say you are suffering from can be cured.—Our Family Medicine Book says the following will do it: "Mix castor oil and brandy together-three ounces of oil to two ounces of brandy and use until relieved." The Sifters have tried the ingredients named, but, owing probably to the fact that they modified the formula somewhat, one of them taking the oil and the other the, brandy, there is a difference of opinion in this office as to the general effect of the medicine.

FROM F. W. A., RICHMOND, TEXAS:

I am a general canvasser for the sale of tombstones, musical instruments, maps, periodical literature, etc., and would like to add your paper to my list of novelties. What are your terms?

TEXAS SIFTINGS

You will see our terms quoted at the head of the *fourth page. We have read the circular you enclose, but we are at a loss to understand whether you sell tombstones, and throw in musical instruments, maps, etc., as an inducement to people to buy tombstones, or whether you sell the maps and things, and throw in a tombstone as a sort of chromo. In any case, however, you are engaged in a noble calling—alleviating the grief and despondency of the disconsolate and bereaved ones with maps and musical instruments, while at the same time you are prepared to tranquilize and restrain the giddy and thoughtless by selling them tombstones. Go on with your good work, and if you think that subscribing to Texas Siftings will sooth the sorrow of bereaved relatives, when they buy a tombstone, you can let them have the paper at $2 a year, and you retain agent's commission. Or, if you will agree to make a specialty of soliciting for subscribers to Siftings, we might arrange with you on such terms that you could afford to give a tombstone as a premium to sub-agents who would get up clubs. Let us hear from you again.*

FROM CARRIE W., FORT WORTH, TEXAS: Can you give me a recipe for removing freckles?

We have been asked that question about a hundred times, and as public journalists, we felt that it would never do to display ignorance regarding the character and habits of the freckle. So we gave one remedy after another—a new one every time—until we went through our family medicine book, taking receipts as they came. Our experiments have been very exhaustive—to the patient. Sometimes we tried kidney wort; to another anxious inquir-

222 er we recommended what our medicine book said would eradicate dandruff from the scalp, and, in another desperate case, we prescribed a remedy that had testimonials certifying that it would draw the core out of a soft corn; but none of our patients ever wrote back and told us that they had suffered with freckles for fourteen years, but that, thanks to one application of our wonderful remedy they were now able to walk without assistance, etc., etc. So we presume our remedies were not quite successful, and in future our medical practice will be confined to answering questions regarding the removal of warts and superfluous hair. We have concluded that freckles that won't yield to such treatment as we prescribed, have settled down to stay.

FROM SAM McN., MINNEAPOLIS:

I am seeking a dry climate for my health. Would you be so kind as to answer through your correspondence column, and tell me what kind of weather you have at this season in Texas. A prompt and concise reply will be appreciated.

BREVITIES

The Gonzales *Inquirer* has a long article about "what shall we do with the ant?" Take it off.

The stage robbers out. West seem to have given up their attempt to ferret out the authorities.

"There will be no more parting there," said the man when he looked into the mirror after having his hair shingled.

A most disgraceful affair recently occurred in Kansas.

Two prominent politicians fought a duel and neither of them was hurt.

Sappho did not assault the editor when she struck the lyre.

Never kick a poor friendless tramp away from your door. Tell a policeman to do it.

The Republican who is kicked straight out of a post office, immediately ceases to be a straight out Republican.

There are no printers in the Texas Penitentiary at Huntsville, notwithstanding that it is so easy to get proof in the case of a printer.

We are gratified to learn that Professor Tice, the weather prophet, is 80 years of age. We will soon get some weather we can depend on.

They make paint of the ancient Egyptian mummies found at Thebes, and too much paint makes the modern women look like ancient Egyptian mummies.

The London *Spectator* says: "Genius protects itself." *224* The *Spectator* has probably heard of the purchase we lately made of a self-cocking revolver.

A circus is heading for Texas. A circus is a great comfort to parents. As long as the circus is in town they know for certain where their boys spend their evenings.

The most truthful and unobtrusive man in the community, will, in one week after he becomes the owner of a setter dog, develop into a talented, gaudy and ostentatious liar.

A Kentucky editor says: "We are not responsible for the article in our inside. It was contributed by a friend," etc. In Texas it is the barkeeper who is responsible for what is in many of the editors' insides.

The Paris Press says that: "Before leaving, Rev Ebenezer Pentecost filled his appointment." Queer name for a flask—what did he fill it with—milk, eh? Did he give you a parting pull at his appointment?

A late fashion note says: "Surah and foulard nightdresses are becoming bouffant." For a long time we have feared that something of that sort would happen to that kind of a night shirt, but we hated to say anything about it.

FASHION NOTES

Freckles will be much worn this summer.

Tan-color is much in vogue, especially in the country.

Face powders grow in popularity, and are sold by all druggists.

There is a decided tendency toward the carrying of fans—to bed.

Heavy plaid shawls and fur jackets are being used everywhere—by moths.

The fashionable ladies' husbands wear shirts without buttons. They pin their collars on behind with a nail.

The hair is now worn box-plaited and shirred with bouffant trimmings behind, and when lawn-tennis lambrequins, cut bias, are hung over the ears, it is considered quite dressy.

Fashionable mottoes for pillow shams are "Goodnight," "Bon Soir," "Did you forget to lock the front door?" "Sweetly Dream," and "Be sure and leave the milk pitcher out."

The latest fashion in art work is fly specks on old china.

Light blue milk with fly insertion is much in vogue 226 at afternoon hotel "teas."

There is a revival this season of prickly heat, and mosquito bars are being much used.

There is a growing inclination among fashionable people to put down low-necked dresses.

Among the ladies, newspapers, slashed and cut bias, with decollette margins, are much used at all seasons.